The Life of a Kamikaze pilot

KAMIKAZE takes you into the life of a young
Japanese pilot who served with the suicide
squadrons organized to destroy the United
States Navy in 1944 and '45. Yasuo Kuwahara was fifteen when he went into the Air
Force, seventeen when the war ended. In this
revealing book, he describes the merciless
ordeal of his basic training, the thrill of his
first air combat. Then, as the war turned
against Japan, he saw his friends fly out,
one by one, on Kamikaze missions of certain
death, received the final order himself, and
survived only by one of the cruelest miracles
in the history of war.

KAMIKAZE

Yasuo Kuwahara
and
Gordon T. Allred

BALLANTINE BOOKS • NEW YORK

Copyright © 1957 by Gordon T. Allred

All rights reserved. Published in the United States by Ballantine Books, a division of Random House, Inc., New York, and simultaneously in Canada by Random House of Canada, Limited, Toronto, Canada.

Library of Congress Catalog Card Number: 58-6911

ISBN 0-345-30485-3

Manufactured in the United States of America

First Ballantine Books Edition: December 1957
Sixth Printing: May 1982

*To the future friendship
of Japan and America*

CONTENTS

Part Six

Part Seven

KAMIKAZE

FOREWORD

Clean-cut, typically reserved and polite, he was only twenty-six when we met at Camp Kobe the summer of 1955. Had it not been for a certain indescribable depth to his eyes, I would have judged him to be even younger. It was definitely the eyes—eyes that had seen such fantastic things that gave him an older quality.

Thenceforth, until my departure from Japan ten months later, I saw a lot of Yasuo Kuwahara, and came to respect him as a friend, a man of integrity. Tragic and violent though his experiences had been, Kuwahara seemed to derive satisfaction from relating them. Not that he was a publicity hound—far from it. But locked within that man was experience that needed telling—experience that might enhance understanding among men and nations. We both believed that.

Surely *Kamikaze* (The Divine Storm) must have been the strangest sort of war ever waged—over five thousand men converted by their country into human bombs—the Japanese suicide pilots, who caused the greatest losses in the history of our navy.

No one will ever comprehend the feelings of those men who covenanted with death. Even condemned convicts don't understand it fully. The convict is atoning for misdeeds; justice is meted out. Of course, there have been heroes from every nation who have deliberately laid down their lives. But where before in all the world has there been such premeditated destruction? Where before have thousands of men diligently set about their own annihilation, mulling over all the details for weeks, sometimes months?

Neither the Shintoistic concept of post-mortal existence as a guardian warrior in the spirit realms, nor the Buddhistic philosophy of Nirvana always provided solace. The "mad, fanatic Jap" was too often a schoolboy, enmeshed in the skein of fate, not above weeping for his mother.

What must it have been like—existing week after week, month after month, when life teetered in the balance with every sweep of the minute hand—never knowing at what minute one's death orders would come?

Obviously, anyone who had completed one of those tragic missions would not be around to tell the tale. But perhaps a very few, through some twist of chance . . . Yes, somewhere there had to be a few—men still warm and alive, who had convenanted with death and the unknown.

It was just such ruminating that led me to seek out Mr. Kuwahara, a resident of Kobe, Honshu, Japan. Daily he recounted his experiences during World War II, and with each discussion I became increasingly fascinated, increasingly awed. For what occurred during his eighteen months in the Imperial Army Air Force seemed too overwhelming to fathom. The life he led—each day of it—I must admit strains credibility all the way.

It is not easy to imagine that Yasuo Kuwahara at only fifteen survived a training program terrible enough to provoke the suicides of nine companions—even that such training could have existed. And who could have imagined that this man, having survived bombings, air battles, and storms, having received his own suicide orders, would be preserved by a horrifying coincidence?

It is this climax, staggering in its irony, that places Mr. Kuwahara in such a singular position today. Among the few remaining *Kamikaze,** his life is unique.

This account appeared in much abbreviated form as a feature story in *Cavalier*, January, 1957. Since that time a number of readers have informed me that the experiences therein are "almost too remarkable to believe." Indeed, one can scarcely escape the feeling that too much happened— not only for a span of eighteen short months, but for an entire lifetime.

Curiously enough, the main problem in writing both the article and this book has been one of deletion. Primarily, it has been a matter of selecting from a great many dramatic events lest the reader become surfeited.

*Plural here. There is no separate designation of the plural in Japanese, and throughout the book the Japanese words that appear are to be understood as singular or plural according to the context.

As to the story's validity: Both Mr. Kuwahara and I have documents attesting all the basic incidents. Witnesses are: Seiji Hiroi of Osaka, a *Kamikaze* pilot who knew the protagonist, and Yoshiro Tsubaki, Yokohama, former commander of the Fourth Squadron at Hiro Air Base, the man who gave Kuwahara his death orders. Both the editors of *Cavalier* and the publishers of Ballantine Books have examined those documents.

But this book is not a compliation of statistics. What is intended here is a human document—an attempt to reveal the thoughts and emotions of a boy who at fifteen was hurled into one of the most awesome, terrifying holocausts of history. It reflects the attitudes, in part, of those who were there with him, as well as the general Japanese outlook on the war.

It is hoped that the reader may experience a certain empathy. If one gains a better appreciation of valor and honor, a keener desire to promote peace, or a little more reverence for life itself this account will be justified.

And the thousands of *Kamikaze*, and the Americans they took with them, whose ashes mingle somewhere in the Pacific . . . those deaths may yet serve a paradoxical but ultimate good for peoples everywhere.

GTA

Part One

PROLOGUE

It is New Year's Day, 1945, at Hiro Air Base in western Honshu. Captain Yoshiro Tsubaki, commander of the Fourth Fighter Squadron, has just called a special meeting. A silence settles over us—only the patter of rain on the roof. The captain has permitted us to sit, while he stands, arms folded, eyes dark and unblinking—seeming to spear us one by one.

After a long time he speaks, sonorously: "The time has at last arrived. We are faced with a great decision."

Again he pauses, but I feel it coming—the fear, greater than I have yet known. Death is there with us, enfolding each man, lingering, growing stronger. And the words from our captain flow so strangely: "Any of you unwilling to give your lives as divine sons of the great Nippon empire will not be required to do so. Those incapable of accepting this honor will raise their hands—now!"

Once more silence and death are almost palpable. The rain has subsided to a soft drizzle. Then, hesitantly, timidly, a hand goes up, then another and another . . . five, six in all. The decision is mine; I can choose to live or die. Hasn't the captain just said so? But somehow . . . Of course, of course, I want to live! But my hands—they remain at my sides trembling. I want to raise them, and I can't. I want to raise my hands; even my soul would have me. Am I a coward? Am I? I cannot do it!

"*Ah, so!*" Captain Tsubaki fixes those who have responded in his stare. "It is good to know early exactly where we stand." They are summoned before us. "Here, gentlemen," he points at the ashen faces, "are six men who have openly admitted their disloyalty. Since they are completely devoid of honor— without spirit—it becomes our duty to provide them with some. These men shall be Hiro's first attack group!"

The breath, held so long within me, struggles out. I want to draw in more air, to expel it with relief, but something clenches inside. Six men from my squadron have just been picked for death. Hiro's first human bombs.

15

NATIONAL GLIDER CHAMPION

It is quite impossible to say where the forces eventuating in Japan's suicide war, the strangest war in history, really originated. Ask the old man, venerable *ojii-san,* with his flowing beard—the man who still wears *kimono* and wooden *geta* on the streets—for he is a creature of the past. Perhaps he will say that these mysterious forces were born with his country over two and a half millennia ago, with Jimmu Tenno, first emperor, descendant of the sun goddess, Amaterasu-Omikami. Or he may contend that their real birth came twenty centuries later, reflected in the proud spirit of the *samurai,* the famed and valiant warriors of feudal times.

Whatever the beginnings, these forces focused upon me in 1943 when I was only fifteen. It was then that I won the Japanese national glider championship.

Back where memory blurs, I can vaguely discern a small boy watching hawks circle over the velvet mountains of Honshu—watching enviously each afternoon. I remember how he even envied the sparrows as they chittered and flitted about the roofs.

Somehow I knew then that my future was waiting somewhere in the sky. At fourteen, attending Onomichi High School, I was old enough to participate in a glider training course sponsored by the Osaka prefecture, a training that had two advantages. First, it was the chance I had waited for all my life—a chance to be in the air. Secondly, the war was reverberating throughout the world, and while many pupils were required to spend part of their regular school time working in the factories, I was permitted to learn glider flying—two hours each day. All students were either directly engaged in producing war materials or preparing themselves as future defenders through such programs as judo, sword fighting, and marksmanship. Even grade school children were taught how to defend themselves with sharpened bamboo shafts.

Our glider training was conducted on a grassy field, and the first three months were frustrating since we never once moved off the ground. Fellow trainees merely took turns towing each other across the lawn, while the would-be pilot vigorously manipulated the wing and tail flaps with hand and foot controls, pretending that he was soaring at some awesome height. A good part of our time was devoted to calisthenics, and it was obvious even then that such preparation was calculated to be more than an interesting pastime. But this I wasn't to comprehend fully until nearly a year later.

Gradually we began taking to the air, only a few feet off the ground at first, but what exhilaration! Eventually we were towed rapidly enough to rise some sixty feet, the maximum height for a primary glider. A scant thirty seconds in the air at best, but it was flying.

Having mastered the fundamentals of the primary glider, we transferred to the secondary, which would remain aloft for several minutes and was car-towed for the take-off. It had a semi-enclosed cockpit, and a control stick with a butterfly-shaped steering device for added control.

Aside from understanding the basic mechanical requirements of glider flying, it was necessary to sense the air currents, to feel them out, automatically judging their direction and intensity, in order to respond instinctively like the hawks above the mountains.

How far should I travel into the wind? Often I could determine this only by thrusting my head from the cockpit. And at times of descent—just before circling to climb with the updrafts—the onrushing air tide seemed so solid as to be stifling. Just before the take-off, the air impact was tremendous, and I needed all my strength to work the controls.

How far to travel in one direction before circling, precisely how much to lift the wing flaps to avoid stalling and still maintain maximum height . . . these things were not plotted on a chart beforehand. But the bird instinct was in me and I was able to pilot my glider successfully enough to qualify for national competition the following year.

Approximately six hundred glider pilots from all of Japan (mainly high school students) had qualified for the event at Mt. Ikoma near Nara, and the competition was divided into two phases: group and individual. Contenders could participate in either or both events and were judged on such points as time in the air, distance traveled at a specified altitude, ability to turn within a designated number of feet, and angle of descent.

Perhaps it was our intensive training, perhaps destiny, that led six of us from Onomichi High School, in western Honshu,

17

to the group championship. Two of our group were selected for individual competition against about fifty others—the best glider pilots in the country. I was one of them.

Each man was to fly four times. Points won during each flight would then be totaled to determine the winner. To my joy and astonishment my first three flights went off almost perfectly. Victory was within sight!

Sunlight was warming the summit of Mt. Ikoma when the final flight began. Fifty yards below, on the immense glider field. I steadied myself in the cockpit, feeling a tremor in the fragile structure that held me—delicate wood covered with silk, curved, and fastened with light aluminum. The tow rope had been attached to a car ahead, a ring in the other end fastened to a hook under the glider's nose. Opening and closing my hand on the control stick, I breathed deeply. "You can do it." I repeated the words and tried to stave off the hollow feeling—the weakness. Simultaneously I began to tingle. This was the biggest test of my life, a chance to be crowned the greatest glider pilot in the empire.

My craft lurched and began sliding across the turf. Moments later I was above Ikoma, feeling the air gush over its dome. Now lifting, straining with the controls, I worked the flaps cautiously to prevent the current from catching under my inner wing.

Then the glider responded to my touch as if it had a life of its own, and I was soaring with the wind, carried on its tide. For a moment I glanced over my shoulder at the landing strip, at the upturned faces, and then began my turn. Three times I circled, rising on the updrafts, then falling. Thirty-eight minutes after the take-off I settled to earth.

Later the judges finished tallying the points and I waited nervously for their verdict. I knew I had done well, that I had a chance. But nothing, just then, seemed real. Suddenly my name was being announced: "Kuwahara, Yasuo— 340 points—first place, individual competition!" Vaguely I heard another name being announced for second place. I felt weak, then strong. Friends were slapping my back, throwing their arms around me—my family, radiant, pushing through the throng. I was glider champion of the Nippon empire.

Little did I realize then that this distinction would soon alter my entire existence.

2

A PREDESTINED DECISION

There had been much ado at the Onomichi train station on my return. Teachers, students, close friends—all were present to congratulate the new champion. The family had held a celebration in my honor. Then, in a few days, my accomplishment was all but forgotten.

Glider training continued, but for the first time in many months I was not looking ahead toward anything special. As the novelty of my championship passed, I grew restless. Life was suddenly drab.

In the evenings after training I wandered homeward with my friends, watching the sun settle beyond the mountains, a red caldron turning the sea to molten steel. Sunset was a special time—a time to have finished the hot bath, to have donned the *yukata* (light-weight, casual *kimono*), to slide the windows back and gaze meditatively, to sit in one's garden contemplating the dark filigree of a mulberry tree against the horizon, to indulge in introspection in the steam rising from a hot cup of *ocha*.

Since early in 1943, however, such times of serenity had begun to fade. Guadalcanal had been lost to the Americans and doubts—the first gray shapes—had come. Not that much had been said . . . but fear came like lingering mist, and the rising sun could not dispel it.

We, who were young, spoke of the war more enthusiastically than the others. My friend, Tatsuno, had a brother in the navy air force who had shot down an American plane, and many evenings this was the subject of conversation as we walked the road from school.

Young as he was, small and almost frail, there was an intensity about Tatsuno, in the way he looked into the sky and spoke of his brother. At times, when the planes passed over, he shook his head saying fervently, "I know he will become an ace. He will bring honor to the emperor." Of course I always agreed. It was comforting to know that our pilots were superior to the enemy, more courageous, that they flew better planes. The radios and newspapers assured us daily of this fact.

19

One of those evenings just after my return from school, a stranger came to our door, and I heard his introduction: "I am Captain Mikami, Hiroyoshi—of the Imperial Army Air Force." A moment later he had removed his shoes and crossed the threshold. The maid, Reiko, having steered him to the western-style reception room, padded quickly off to inform my father.

My father, a contractor and the most affluent man in Onomichi, continued his leisurely bath and directed my mother to entertain the visitor. Later he emerged to execute the formalities of introduction, while mother retired to supervise the maid's preparation of gochiso, the main meal of the day.

Meanwhile, outside the guest room, I waited tensely, knowing that the visit presaged something very important, listened while the captain and my father exchanged the customary pleasantries, politely discussing the irrelevant, punctuating their sentences with a soft sibilance.

"Winter is well upon us," the captain observed.

"Indeed, that is so," my father said, and slurped his ocha in a well-bred manner.

After they had conversed for some time without really saying anything, it was time for gochiso. Mother had planned sukiyaki, and it was taken for granted that Captain Mikami would stay.

As we sat on our cushions around the low, circular table, the maid bustled back and forth while Tomika, my sister probed at the glowing coals in the hibachi. Mother, arranging and sugaring the beef slices, asked, "Where is the shoyu?" The maid skittered toward the kitchen, making plaintive apologies for forgetting the soy sauce.

Covertly I peered at Captain Mikami from time to time, averting my gaze whenever his glittering eyes met mine. Penetrating eyes, unnerving!

All during the meal only the two men spoke, the rest of us merely registering our existence by careful smiles and slight bowings of the head whenever the conversation ran in our direction. I sensed an atmosphere of constraint and realized that both mother and Tomika were apprehensive.

Father and the captain spoke tediously about the war, touching upon conditions at Iwo Jima, Okinawa and other islands. Speaking of Guadalcanal, my father reiterated a notion firmly intrenched in the Japanese mind at that time: that the departure of our troops from that area had merely been a strategic withdrawal—by no means an enemy triumph. Captain Mikami affirmed this and discussed the valor of our men at some length. As to the increased bombing of our homeland, he emphasized another common belief: Our militarists had known perfectly well, all along, that such things would happen, and consequently there was no reason for apprehension. Such things had all been taken into consideration before Pearl Harbor. Inevitable, yes, but we were prepared for them. In fact, we were prepared for any exigency, securely aware that our divine empire would ultimately triumph.

After dinner I was asked to sit with the two men in the guest room, and at long last our visitor's courteous indirection gave way to a military straightforwardness.

Fixing me with his hawk eyes, then turning to father, he said, "You have an honorable son. Your son has gained acclaim that few men of his age have achieved—few of any age. Already he is becoming a man of whom his esteemed father can be proud."

My father tilted his head slightly, sucked at his long-stemmed pipe and murmured appreciation: *"Domo arigato."*

"He is one of whom his country can be proud," the captain continued. "He can bring great honor to the family of Kuwahara." Something began to ferment within me, a sensation like the one I had felt just before my championship flight.

By now the captain was proceeding swiftly. "Our gracious emperor, our honorable leaders at the *Daihonei* Imperial Military Headquarters in Tokyo are, as you know, seeking such young men, men with allegiance to His Imperial Majesty, with talent and devotion for their country. . . . men who will fly like avenging eagles against the enemy."

A brightness shone in father's eyes. "Indeed! It is good that we have such men. The time has come for us to strike with all our strength—like the winds from Heaven!"

"As you may have supposed," the captain went on, "I am a representative, sent here to interview you and your son in behalf of the Imperial Army Air Force!"

Beaming, and with a carefully manufactured surprise, father exclaimed, *"Ah so!"*

Actually, Captain Mikami directed very few remarks to me. I only half-heard his next words regarding the glory of the air force, and enlistment requirements. I sat smiling, feeling my insides turn hot and cold. During those moments it was impossible to assess my own attitude. All my life I had contemplated joining the air force. How many hours, days and nights, had I dreamed of becoming a fighter pilot who knew no fear, who had no equal! How often had I envisioned myself, plummeting from a golden sky to destroy the enemy! How many heroic air battles had Tatsuno and I conjured up together!

But here now was reality. And in the abruptness of reality my mind could not gauge my heart. I had felt mother's uneasiness all during dinner, Tomika's as well. And now I was gripped with foreboding as though their coldness had touched me like a chill wind.

Then the captain addressed me: "What are your feelings in this matter?" That was all he said. I began to speak, then faltered. I couldn't even get the words out. "Take a few minutes to consider," he said, "I will wait."

A few minutes! Suddenly I felt ill. I ran my hands over my face, back over my hair, and felt sweat. The room had become stifling. Smiling wanly, I mumbled, "Excuse me, please. I will get a drink."

I had wanted to tell the captain that I needed no time to consider. No real man ever wavered. No real man ever felt his heart freeze, felt anxiety or a cold soul. In the tradition of the *bushido* (the *samurai* code of chivalry) he spoke of the glory of death, saying, "I go to die for my country. It fills me with humility to have been selected by the emperor." But I . . . I was more boy than man. I wanted my mother.

Quickly I went to her room. It was empty. Softly I called. No answer. Thinking perhaps she was sitting in the cold, by the garden, I slipped out into the night and called again, seeing the moon balanced on the trellis, washing the yard in a faint, luminous glow. Beyond our surrounding walls the dark road stretched, flecked with the occasional red of a lantern. Not a sound.

There was light in an upstairs window, though, and I hastened inside, mounting the steep stairway. There in my room sat Tomika gazing at my picture album. "Where did mother go?" I asked.

Tomika paused. "She went out—to walk."

Carefully I looked at my sister, momentarily forgetting the problem at hand. "What's the matter, Tomika?" Gently I touched her lustrous, black hair. "Is there something?" There in the album was my picture, taken when I had won the glider championship—my own face, warmed in a smile of

22

pride. A tiny drop spattered, blurring that smile. Tomika was crying.

Whenever my sister cried, her round face was transformed into something ethereal. "Tomika," I half-whispered, "Why? You mustn't cry!" Pushing the album aside I sat down beside her. Fiercely Tomika took my hands and squeezed them. Her eyes lifted gradually until they met my own. For a long second we were motionless, looking into each other—till at last Tomika began shaking her head. "My little brother . . . my little brother. . . ."

Something in my throat pained, growing dry and large. It was as if a thumb were pressing against my windpipe. "Tomika," I choked, "what, what can I do?" Suddenly, I clapped my hands over my face, sucking the breath in. That way the tears wouldn't come so easily. Then all at once, her arms were around me, her cheek against mine. "No, no," she kept whispering, "not my little brother. You're only a baby!"

The last words jolted me, and I remembered my friends, especially Tatsuno. What would he think of me—such a maudlin display! Then I thought of the captain downstairs, waiting—impatiently by now, wondering why I was so slow, wondering if I was a coward! These thoughts converged on me all in an instant. I was angry with myself, and with Tomika.

"I'm hardly a baby, Tomika," I mumbled.

She tried to pull me closer, but I drew away. A baby! For an instant I almost hated her. "I'm a man! I'm fifteen years old! Can you call me a baby when I am the best glider pilot in Japan? Don't you realize, Tomika, that I am being honored —by the emperor himself?"

"Yes," she replied softly, "I know well enough. You will even die for the emperor!" Then we were weeping togther.

Moments later I broke away and stumbled down to the sink—to bathe my face in cold water. Then I looked at my eyes in the mirror—bloodshot, my face weak and distressed. Horrified, I doused my face once more, then patted it dry with a towel.

Embarrassed, but as resolute as possible, I returned to my father and the captain. I entered, smiling and bowing, wondering all the while whether they detected my weakness. Both men observed me in utter silence. Momentarily I hesitated, and the captain raised an eyebrow.

I struggled, faltering. It was as though I were on the brink

23

of an abyss, hemmed in by enemies, knowing that there was no alternative but to jump or be pushed.

It was my father who pushed: "Well, my son?"

Bowing to the captain, I stammered, "I am greatly honored, sir. I will be proud to accept your generous offer, in behalf of our esteemed emperor."

"Good," he said simply, and produced the enlistment forms for us to read over. Woodenly I went from word to word, not even understanding them. "Kuwahara-*san*," the captain addressed father, "you will kindly sign here. Your son will sign here."

"*Sodes*," father grunted. "It's so." And he appeared to be reading intently. He pointed a slender, tan finger at the print and sucked air in through his teeth. "Hiro Air Force Base?"

"*Ha*," Captain Mikami grinned, and they both looked at me to note my reaction. Yes, I was pleased. In fact, I suddenly felt much better. Hiro was less than fifty miles away.

Father arose and got his special, wooden stamp. He pressed it against the ink pad, then against the forms. There—an indelible, orange oval against the tissue paper—"Kuwahara," never to be removed. When I had signed my own name to it, the formalities were completed.

It was time for Captain Mikami to leave, and we accompanied him to the door. "You have made a wise decision," he informed me. We bowed, exchanging *sayonara*, and he drifted quickly into the night.

Once he had gone, my being in the air force somehow seemed less a reality. It would be three months until my departure. . . a long time. For some time my father and I sat talking. Father had been an army lieutenant years before, and he began relating some of his honorable experiences.

Shigeru, one of my older brothers, was with the army Counter-Intelligence in Java, while the other, Toshifumi, was a dentist in Tokyo who had not yet been inducted. "It is good to have worthy sons in the service of their nation and family," father said. "And you, Yasuo, will bring the greatest honor of all." We sat near the window, watching the sky. Father's hand slipped over my shoulder. A transport plane passed over, blinking red and green, the alternation of colors making it appear to rock strangely along its course. We watched until it faded, listening as the purr became more muffled.

"Perhaps in a few months you may be piloting a Suisei bomber."

"I would like to be a fighter pilot," I replied, "more than anything else."

"Ah ha! That's exactly what I thought! Yes . . . yes, that would be good," he agreed. "That would be best of all. There is something unique about a fighter pilot. He is the true *samurai*. His airplane is his sword. It becomes his very soul. The fighter pilot must work with others as part of a team, but he also has the best chance to be an individualist." Father paused. "Yes, I am sure you must become a fighter pilot, Yasuo. He can do more for the emperor than a thousand foot soldiers. With courage he can gain great honor, perhaps more than anyone else in the military. And you do have courage, Yasuo, my son." His hand gripped my shoulder, and I felt him looking at me.

"I hope so, my father," I said.

"You have courage, son, you have courage!" His hand clamped my shoulder more tightly. "The Kuwaharas have always had courage. No one has more noble ancestors."

"That is so," I acknowledged, and studied his profile for an instant: a strong chin tilting slightly upward, a nose that curved down, eyes that seemed to catch a glow from the sky.

"You will defend your home and your country, and you will see the day when the Western powers are driven back across the Pacific, for you will help to drive them. Perhaps you may be among those who will conquer America. The Imperial Way will sweep like a tide across that land."

"It may take many months," I said hesitantly. "The West has big armies and navies, many aircraft. Is it not true?"

"That is true," father admitted. "That is true. And it will not be accomplished in a day. But bear in mind, Yasuo, that physical size and material might are always secondary. It is the determination of *Yamatodamashii* that counts. Consider the thousands of Americans we have taken prisoner . . . thousands of them!"

Shifting, he drummed his fingers gently on my shoulder and asked very confidentially, "And how many of our men have surrendered to the Americans?"

How proud I was to converse with father on such significant matters—almost as an equal!

"Very few."

"A mere handful! You see? The Americans lose a few men and they become terrified. They are eager to surrender. Our prison camps are full to the brim with cowardly Americans.. Of course, some of them are brave. It is foolish to underestimate an enemy . . . But let us look at it this way, Yasuo. Suppose for a moment that one hundred American infantrymen were pitted against a much larger force of our own men on a small island. How many of those Americans would have to be killed before the rest would surrender? How many?"

"Not more than ten, I would guess."

Father shook his head slightly. "No, it would probably take more than ten, possibly twenty-five or thirty. However, supposing the conditions were reversed—how many of our own soldiers would need to be killed before the rest would surrender?"

"They would never surrender!"

"So, you see? The only Japanese ever taken captive, with rare exceptions, are those who have been wounded so severely that they cannot move, or those who have lost consciousness from loss of blood. It is not merely a matter of physical and material strength. It is a matter of courage, determination . . . spiritual strength! It is for this reason that Japan will eventually triumph. Do you understand, my son?"

"Yes, my father."

3

WINTER AND THE WANING DAYS

At school the following day I was quick to inform my friends of the honor that had come. Once again I became someone important. During lunch period, I barely had time to eat the *sushi* cakes in my *bento* (lunch box.) Schoolmates clustered about, pressing me with questions.

"Did he come right to your home?" someone asked.

"Yes," I replied. "He stayed for several hours and had dinner with us."

Kenji Furuno, one of the better glider students, plied me with one question after another. "Did he just come right out and ask you? What did he do? Did he tell you that you had to?"

"He asked me, of course," I answered. "Naturally we discussed the matter at some length with my father."

"What did the captain say, though?" Kenji persisted. "I mean did he just say, 'Will you please be so kind as to honor the Imperial Air Force with your presence?'" Several students laughed rather excitedly.

I failed to join them, however. Kenji had suddenly become someone a bit inferior—along with the rest of them. "Hardly," I told him. "Captain Mikami told me that I had been chosen to serve His Imperial Majesty."

"Didn't he even give you any time to decide?" a younger student asked, "not even a day or two?"

Almost unconsciously I eyed him, as the captain had eyed me the night before. His smile wavered. "Would you need time to decide a thing like that?" I said.

"Well . . . I suppose not," he stammered.

Tatsuno had been eating quietly, listening. Sometimes his thoughts seemed more like those of an old man than a high school student. "I don't think anyone would turn down such an honor," he said. "I doubt if anyone would dare to. Myself, I want to be a pilot like my brother, more than anything else in the world. Just the same, when you think about it . . . After all, he's going . . . Well, no one knows for sure whether he'll ever come back."

"That is true," I admitted and sucked my lips together. Everyone was silent for a moment, either staring at his own feet or out the windows. Then it was time for noon classes to begin.

I went through the next class in almost a trance. It was as if I had been strangely set apart from the world. Old Tanaka-*sensei*, the instructor, the students . . . even the desks, the books and the dark walls . . . Everything seemed different. I was seeing and listening with an indescribable objectivity. Somewhere out in the white afternoon a plane kept droning, the sound barely perceptible. At times it seemed only an echo in my imagination, but it made me tingle.

When it came time for glider training, I participated with zeal, performing every act with precision. Quite suddenly I decided that from that time on I would make no mistakes during glider flying—not a single mistake, however small. This habit of perfection would then be so well established

27

that within a few months I would learn to fly a real plane just as perfectly. I would be the perfect pilot. I would shoot down a thousand enemy planes. And there would come a time when the name of Kuwahara would ring throughout all Japan. On the emperor's birthday I would be chosen to perform stunts in the skies over Tokyo while millions of people cheered below. Later I would be escorted across the green moat, over the arching wooden bridge. I would gaze down at the lily pads, the snowy swan, and the great, listless carp. Then I would enter the palace of the emperor—the Imperial Palace, where the emperor himself would present me with the *Kinshi Kunsho,* the coveted medal of honor, after the order of the Golden Kite.

Such dreams of glory were still with me when I returned home in the evening. We scuffed along the dirt road, and for a time we were silent, enjoying the sound of our wooden *geta.* Eventually Tatsuno, guessing my thoughts, remarked, "You know, Yasuo, if you weren't the best friend I ever had, I could be very envious now."

After a moment's silence I replied, "Tatsuno-*kun,* I'd give anything if we were going in together." I clapped my hand on his narrow shoulder. "Believe me, Tatsuno, I truly would."

Tatsuno threw his arm around me and we scuffed along together. "You know, there's a very good chance that you . . ." I hesitated. "I mean I wouldn't be surprised if you got the same chance, any day now."

But he shook his head: "Oh, I don't think so. I doubt it. After all, look who you are! You're the national glider champion!"

"That doesn't prove a thing," I shrugged. "Anyway, you're a good pilot yourself. You went to the finals. Besides, there wouldn't be many fliers in the Imperial Air Force if they picked only one glider champion every year, would there?" Tatsuno was silent. "Would there?" I insisted, and began shaking him back and forth trying to pull him off balance. Still he wouldn't answer, but a grin was starting. "Would there?"

Suddenly I pushed the long visor of his school cap over his eyes. "Would there!" That did it. He laughed and grabbed for my own cap. Then we were cavorting along, taking swipes at each other, laughing, and out *geta* clattered loudly along the paved streets near home.

Moments later we had said good-by and I entered my home

to find mother hunched over a book—rather a startling scene, since she rarely read. I greeted her a bit dubiously.

"Hello, Yasuo," she replied.

"Is father home yet?"

She answered quickly: "No."

"Is he still at work?"

"No, he is not! I don't think he will be home tonight."

Then I knew. It was never easy for her—not after all these years. Her veined hands folded the book, and she looked silently at the cover—*Tale of Genji*. "My mother gave me this book when I was a young girl," she said. "I still remember—almost all of it."

"Yes, yes, it's a good book," I told her. Sitting beside her I decided to broach the matter: "No one could ever take your place. You know how much father loves you, mother."

"Oh, yes," she answered, shaking her head. "Your father loves me. It's just that . . . just that I'm not so young any more—not like his Kimiko, and his Toshiko, and all the others." For an instant she smiled wistfully. "There was a time when your father never looked at another woman. He wasn't the only man who thought I was beautiful."

"You're still beautiful! I think you're the most beautiful woman in the whole world!"

Reddening faintly, mother said, "I must think Yasuo is a full-grown man now—talking such foolishness." Then she kissed my cheek. "Of course, your father loves me. He will return tomorrow. And my children love me. That's my greatest joy."

There was little to be said in such a moment. It was a Japanese man's prerogative to have his concubines, so long as he could afford them. *Geisha* girls are not prostitutes, but father went to see one regularly. This I had learned from my older brothers. She was his wife away from home.

Japanese women differ from Western women in many ways. For one thing they usually show greater deference to the opposite sex. And even today, although less servile, they rarely contradict their men. They occupy a subordinate role, acknowledging the husband as master and maker of decisions. Obedience is one of the female's most important characteristics—according to the male.

So it was that whenever my father went away, my mother continued quietly about her business in the home. This verbal expression of her feelings was highly irregular so far as I was

29

concerned. Possibly it stemmed from her awareness that I would soon be leaving home. Usually when father made a "business" trip, only the silence, the wearied expression, betrayed mother's emotions. Upon returning, father was invariably gruff and unapproachable—a feeble disguise for his guilt, a guilt he never overcame despite the convenient *mores*.

In a way, however, I enjoyed having father leave. Not that I didn't love him. I simply felt less restrained when he was away. It gave me an opportunity to be alone with mother and Tomika, to be the center of attention. As the weeks faded, and as the time for my departure approached, I took increasing comfort in being alone with them.

It was Tomika, most of all, who made my departure almost agonizing. She had been more than a sister, always standing up for me against my older brothers. It was Tomika, as well as mother, who washed my clothes, cooked my favorite foods, and fondly indulged me.

Often, as the time drew short, we wandered by the wintry ocean, along the cold sands that smelled of salt and fish. On those rare days in January, when the sun parted the clouds, we gathered shells and listened to the coughing of junks in the harbor. Even when the weather was cold, men and women bustled about in the long dingy shacks, smoking fish. Aged people, crinkled and brown, in tattered clothing, hunched along the beach over their nets.

I had never known their privation or gone shoeless and halfclad like their children, and there seemed to be something pleasant about their life—its utter simplicity. Sometimes we watched those fisher people spread a catch of tiny, shimmering fish to dry in woven baskets. When sunlight warmed the beach they would rest long enough to dig their bare toes into the sand, and their voices were always mild—totally unlike the boisterous clamor of town.

There was a timelessness, a quiet, about the ocean people that made the war seem very unreal. The enemy had bombed parts of our homeland, but this too seemed unreal—like something that happened only in books or movies.

The same peace could be felt as we walked among the farms further back along the mountains, viewing the terraced slopes. During the winter the fields and paddys were bleak and lifeless, but with the coming of spring they exploded into emerald. The rice pushed higher and higher from the muck and held its greenness all during the summer, while the mountains, cloaked in their own deep foliage, brooded darker and darker as the months moved on.

But with startling abruptness my three months had fled. All at once I realized that the days with my family and friends would soon be gone, perhaps forever. Perhaps I might never return to Onomichi. Near the end of January, when Tomika and I sat in my upstairs room one afternoon, the sense of finality hit me hard. Leaving tomorrow! The thought was both exciting and frightening, making me uneasy, unable to concentrate. I was hovering on the verge of something momentous, something no words could describe.

Gazing toward the mountains, I murmured restlessly, "I wish it were summer; then we could go hiking and swimming again."

"Yasuo," Tomika replied, "can this really be? Is there really a war? Are there people who hate us, who want to conquer us?"

"Why not?" I answered. "We hate them. We want to conquer them, don't we?" The Allies were big people, pale-skinned, with strange hair. Red hair, some of them—others yellow. They were selfish, prodigal and lazy, wallowing in luxury. Their soldiers were savaged and guttural-voiced. "Do you believe what they say about the American marines, that they are required to kill and eat their grandmothers? That's what half the people are saying at school."

"No," Tomika said firmly, "that's silly! No one would ever do a thing like that."

No doubt the Caucasian concept regarding us was just as extreme. To the average American we were yellow-skinned, slant-eyed monkeys, dwelling in paper houses. We had no spark of originality. We could only copy. Our soldiers—indeed, every Japanese, including Japanese-Americans—were considered sneaky, treacherous and fanatic. "Dirty Jap" was a popular epithet, I am told. Often I have wondered since just how much such forms of ignorance (on both sides) have ultimately contributed to wars.

In January of 1944, however, I didn't ponder such problems deeply. I had been reared to believe that the Imperial Way of Righteousness and Truth was the best way—the only way—and that it would eventually envelop the world. In time all nations of the earth would be united in a huge hierarchy, with Japan at the head. Apparently such a condition could not be achieved without a war. Then too, with a

31

rapidly increasing population and little room to expand we were in dire need of more territory.

Still, I couldn't really make myself hate the enemy. As I sat with Tomika, meditating, I wanted only to live and let live. Nevertheless, I felt the growing tension and excitement. Before long I would be flying a real plane. This alone would make me a hero in the eyes of all my friends in Onomichi.

During my final days at home the sense of reality had steadily increased. Through with my studies now, I had said good-by to my teachers and school friends. It was comforting, at this point, to learn that two other students had already been selected for the air force, that Tatsuno was one of them. He was to enter later, and both of us were overjoyed at the prospect. During those last days, we were together frequently. Our common bond with the air force brought us even closer, until we were like brothers. When Tatsuno first told me the good news I clapped him on the back, exclaiming, "See, what did I tell you!" Tatsuno had only smiled faintly— the wise old man in a boy's body. But I knew that he was thrilled.

On my last day at home I called on him, visited a few other friends, then spent the remaining hours with my family. Father was obviously proud, talking with me more intimately than ever before, while mother and Tomika prepared special *sushi* (rice) dishes, *sashimi* (sliced, raw fish) and various delicacies for me.

Before midnight I bade my family a good rest and crawled in beneath my quilted *futon*. But for many hours sleep didn't come. My thoughts were a revolving kaleidoscope of memories, visions of the future, and apprehensions. One special fear possessed me. I was a year, even two years, younger than most of the boys who entered military service. Would I be able to keep up with them? How would I withstand the rigorous routine, the punishment I had heard so much about?

In a state of half-sleep I tossed and squirmed for a while. Then I slipped back to reality. Some planes had just passed overhead, and were purring off into the night. Sitting beside me, softly stroking my forehead, was my mother. I extended my hand and felt the warmth of her own. In the dark there came a faint sound, and I knew that Tomika was there too. Then my thoughts settled, and sleep came.

Part Two

4

INSTILLING THE SPIRIT

Hiro Air Force Base was only two hours' train ride from my home, but it was an entirely different world.

I had been warned what to expect, and had tried to prepare myself. But no man could possibly condition himself for what lay in store at Hiro.

Sixty of us, all new men, were assigned to four of the base's forty-eight barracks. Hiro itself was some three miles in circumference, enclosing a long, narrow airstrip running the full length of the base. It also contained a training ground, school, dispensary, storage houses, plus a variety of buildings and offices.

On one side of the airstrip were assembly plants, and a fighter-plane testing area. At that stage of the war Japan was in dire need of money and materials—particularly aluminum. By then the assembly lines were being run by schoolboys, and about five of every thirty planes constructed eventually fell apart, sometimes in mid-air.

Before being assigned our quarters we received an orientation lecture from one of the *hancho* (NCO's—sergeants in our case.) We were instructed carefully how to make beds, how to display our clothes, how to have our boots and shoes polished to a glossy finish at all times. Perfect orderliness—and complete cleanliness—were rigidly demanded. Further, we were told that *Shoto Rappa* (Taps) would sound at 9 P.M.

Obligations in such matters were not much different from those in any other country. Military men, regardless of nationality, follow the same basic rues. The great difference lay in how these rules were enforced. An American, for example, who failed to be cleanshaven or to have his shoes properly shined for an inspection might have his pass revoked for a day or two, or he might be given extra duty.

For us, however, as for all of Nippon's basic trainees, the slightest infraction, the most infinitesimal mistake, brought excruciating punishment. What I can describe only as a siege of ruthless discipline and relentless castigation began in the first hours of our arrival, and thereafter never ceased during all the days of our training—a siege so terrible that some did not survive it.

American prisoners of war, "victims of Japanese atrocities," generally fared no worse than we did. Some, in fact, received milder treatment. Allied men, such as those incarcerated at Umeda and Osaka, operated their own makeshift dispensaries and received better medical treatment than many of our own men. Many of those Americans, forced to unload ships and trains, managed to smuggle away great quantities of food not only for themselves, but also for the guards over them in return for co-operation and silence.

True, by their own standards, they were severely mistreated but no more than we trainees. No matter how perfectly we performed our tasks, the *hancho* found excuses to make us suffer. Punishment was an integral part of our training and served two main purposes: to create unwavering discipline, and to develop an invincible fighting spirit.

For all of us it was a question not merely of learning skills but of survival. Anyone who could withstand the *hancho* for three months would never run from an enemy, and would prefer death to surrender.

Whether this policy really produced a superior fighting man, I am not prepared to say. Courage may have more than one connotation. Nonetheless, it did create men who were either so fearless or so dedicated that they would almost invariably fight to the death. The enemy was aware that until the latter stages of the war only one of our men for every hundred killed was ever taken captive. And usually captives were taken only after they had been severely wounded or had fainted from their wounds.

As if watching a film, I see now the scared, homesick boy I was that first night in the air force. I lay on my bunk feeling like a trapped rabbit, trying to imagine what the training would ultimately be like, wondering what the next day would bring. Anxiety had left me weak and too nervous to sleep.

Suddenly our door burst open. The *shuban kashikan* (NCO's in charge of quarters) were making their first inspection. Tense, breathless, I listened to their muttering, watched the yellow play of their flashlights. I realized that all fifteen men in the barrack, like myself, were hanging in suspense. We all must have prayed that the *shuban kashikan* would depart, but our prayers were not answered.

The room lights flashed on and we were driven from our beds with slaps, kicks and commands: "Outside, you boobs! Outside, mamma's little boys!"

Dazed and blinking I arose, and a heavy hand cuffed me. "Hey, baldy," someone said, referring to my shorn head, "move out!" A violent shove, and I was booted out the door.

Clad in nothing but our *fundoshi* (loin cloths), we were lined up along the barrack and a fat *hancho* began cursing us —our first meeting with Master Sergeant Noguchi, "The Pig." "Did you all live like beasts at home?" he railed. "Or have you just decided to live that way now that you're away from your mothers? You were warned today about keeping your quarters neat. Apparently you thought we were only talking to hear ourselves—*soka?*" For a while he eyed us silently. "Uh huh!" he grinned slyly, "they don't even know how to stand at attention." For a moment he looked almost like a reproving father. "Green kids," he chuckled and shook his head. I breathed with relief. Maybe training wouldn't be so tough. Maybe they had a different policy now. . . .

The Pig motioned to one of the *hancho* and winked. A moment later the *hancho* handed him a ball bat. "Thank you very much." He spoke the words ever so politely. Suddenly I realized that here was a man who was the perfect master at handling recruits, that he knew all the problems and relished his job. Smiling crookedly at us, he pointed to an inscription on the bay. "Do you know what this says?" Silence. "It says, '*Yamatodamashii Seishinbo.*'" We knew the meaning well enough—a ball bat for instilling the Japanese fighting spirit.

"Do you know what this is for?" he demanded.

"Yes, sir," one or two of us murmured.

"Oh, tsk! tsk!" He looked compassionate, distressed. "Didn't you have enough to eat? Why, boys, I could barely hear you. Now, seriously, don't you really know the significance of this lovely bat?" Most of us answered that time, but still very timidly.

"Oh, come now! That was no louder than someone farting in the bath. How long since your mother stopped suckling you?" A high giggle burst from him and he shook his head at one of the grinning *hancho*. "Green kids! Tell me the truth, Sakigawa, have you ever seen such green little bastards?" The *hancho* leered, and on or two of us smiled faintly. "Wipe

35

off those smiles!" The Pig roared. "Go on! Wipe them off!"

Halfheartedly we passed our hands over our mouths, staring at him wide-eyed. At this he cackled almost uncontrollably. For some time he shook with mirthless laughter, then wiped his eyes moaning, "Oh God, I've been in this business too long!"

Stifling little sobs of hilarity, he said, "I fear we shall have to begin your training. About face!" We turned facing the barrack, to see a metal bar, waist-high, running the length of the building. We were ordered to bend forward and grasp the bar with both hands. Again we heard the maniacal laughter. "Look at those poor little asses!" Almost a satanic glee. Then he gained control of himself. "All right, boys—we shall now put some spirit into you!"

Those words filled me with terror, and I battled the desire to break and run. There was a smack, and the first man in line gasped and grabbed his rear. Two *hancho* had moved in with bats. "Keep hold of the bar!" one of them snarled. The victim grabbed on and writhed as the bat fell again. "Stand still!" The bat fell a third time. The sound of wood striking flesh drew closer and closer, the grunts of pain more immediate. Those who uttered the slightest sound received additional blows.

Grinding my teeth, I gripped the bar with all my might, blinking at the wall before me. The man on my left was now getting the treatment. For one frightening moment I waited. Then—my whole body jolted—a white flash, fire shooting through my buttocks and up my back. Never in my life had I felt such pain. But somehow I managed to remain silent and almost motionless. Perhaps it was because I'd had more time than some of the others to prepare myself.

The man with the bat paused, his eyes upon my quivering back. He moved on.

At last the treatment was over and we were herded into the barrack. As we tossed and groaned on our cots, the door opened once again. Every one fell silent. "Not again! Not again!" I thought, and the words kept pounding in my head. Our friend, The Pig, was lounging in the doorway, the light cutting across his puffy face. For some time he remained that way, dragging on a cigarette, expelling the smoke through his nostrils. I lay on my stomach, hugging the mattress, watching the smoke spiral up past the porch light.

At last he flicked the butt into a trash can and called, almost kindly, almost conspiratorily, "Hey, now do you know what the bats are for?"

"Yes, sir!" Every man in the barrack bellowed the words. Chuckling, he quietly closed the door.

5

TAIKO BINTA—A SPLENDID GAME

The following morning The Pig assembled us for a lecture. Gravely he said, "From now on I want you men to regard me as an older brother. If you have any questions or requests or problems I hope that you will bring them to me. That's what I'm here for."

It was hard to believe that this was the same man who had been terrorizing and beating us only eight hours before. There was a dignity about him, an understanding. All at once I wanted to like The Pig. I even felt ashamed that he had been dubbed with such a name. I wanted to go to him with my troubles, to hear words of understanding.

"Now I know," he continued, "that you have all heard that air force training is an unpleasant experience. It doesn't need to be, not if you do what you are told. Just do everything you are told; it's very simple."

He concluded his lecture saying, "The time has now come for you to become men. As men you will soon carry the weight of your country, the weight of the world, on your shoulders. So—among other things—you must learn to follow instructions implicitly! Immediately! Do not worry about the reasons for any instructions. They are given because they are right! We are the head. You are the arms and legs. Now yesterday, you were given careful instructions regarding neatness in the barracks. You failed to comply. In one barrack a shoe was missing! In two others, ash trays were not centered properly upon the tables. If further infractions of this sort occur I shall be compelled to give you *real* punishment."

He paused to survey us, then glanced knowingly at the other two *hancho*, his assistants. "What you got last night wasn't anything at all. You weren't hurt. But by the time you finish training under *Hancho* Noguchi, you will be able to withstand anything. You will be able to laugh when a little thing like a ball bat is laid across your rear. I will make men of you!"

The training schedule itself was reasonable enough. We rose at six for the formation ten minutes later. We then had twenty minutes of calisthenics and running before morning mess. We were fed well, our diet consisting mainly of fish, rice, and bean soup—brought from the mess hall to our individual barracks in great wooden "honey buckets." Our eating utensils were bowls and chopsticks.

After breakfast, we were briefed by the officer of the day, and then given further instructions by The Pig. Except for noon mess, the remainder of the morning and afternoon was spent in class instruction, calisthenics, combat training, and glider practice. From 4:00 until 6:00 P.M. we scrubbed our barracks and shaped up all our equipment and clothing for the dreaded nightly inspection. In addition, we had to keep the *hancho* quarters in order, wash and iron their clothes.

After evening mess we had a critique by The Pig which lasted from thirty minutes to two hours. The remainder of the time was our own, until just before 9:00 P. M., when we had a formation roll call before the barracks. Shortly thereafter we were in our cots, the lights out.

Such was the schedule of training. But it was in the administration of this routine that our lives were translated to nightmares. Yes, lights went out at nine, but it was then that the *shuban kashikan* made their rounds, and it was a rare night that they didn't find something wrong, regardless of our efforts to keep the barracks in a state of perfection.

A few nights after our first acquaintance with the ball bats we were taught an interesting game called *Taiko Binta*, all because one trainee had removed another's shoe brush from its proper place.

After we had been herded into the cold, wearing only our *fundoshi*, The Pig leered at us and said, "All right, my little darlings. You have failed to heed my warning. . . . You, over there! Stand at attention!" He struck an idiotic pose, slumped, belly distended, arms dangling apelike. A few of us smiled faintly, and The Pig, fully appreciating his role, proceeded to assume other weird postures. Pointing at various men, he would caricature their stance and expression, tilting his nose upward, bulging his eyes, or staring straight ahead in mock terror.

38

Under better circumstances The Pig would have been quite a comedian. I never ceased to be amazed at his dual personality. He was totally unpredictable. Only a few moments after these antics he subjected us to a new sadistic punishment.

"Tonight," he purred, "we will all take part in a new game, a pleasant little game really—*Taiko Binta!*" His grin faded as he snapped, "Give me two ranks!" Swiftly we complied. "First rank! About face!" Now two ranks of seven trainees each stood facing each other, with an extra man left over.

Approaching the extra The Pig said, "Now I shall demonstrate." Standing directly before the pallid youth he purred, "We are now adversaries." Then more loudly: "The object of the game is simply—this!" Swift as a ferret his fist struck. The boy cried out and fell to the ground clutching his face.

A murmur flowed through the ranks. "Silence!" The Pig shrilled. "As you can see, the game is very simple. The object is to alternate blows—give and take. Unfortunately my teammate is a poor player. Look! He has collapsed like a puny girl! So, much as I hate to do so, I must withdraw from the game."

The boy lay where he had fallen, still holding his face, rolled up like a snail as though he might thus escape from the world. Then the Pig prodded him to his feet and solicitously helped him to the sidelines. He then commanded that the game begin, directing the men in the first rank to strike the faces of those in the second.

"Now, first rank—on the count of three." He counted as sweetly as any mother putting her baby to bed: "*Ichi, ni, san* —strike!" Apathetically the blows began. "A little harder!" our *hancho* intoned. "A little harder! Ha! You hit like butterflies! You are going to force me to demonstrate again, boys." The first blows hadn't bothered me much, but soon they began to hurt, even though my opponent was pulling his punches. As the pain increased, we in the second rank backed away, and thereby gave the other two *hancho* an excuse to wield their bats. While they struck at us from the rear, The Pig cried, "Ha! You hit like butterflies, too, you *hancho!* Give me that bat, Kakuda!" Chuckling, he scuttled along behind us, delivering rapid, chopping strokes. I lurched forward, causing my opponent's blow to land much harder than he intended it to. My nose went numb and I swallowed as the warm trickle began in my throat. At last it was time to alternate.

I was making my blows as light as possible, when one of the sharp-eyed *hancho* noticed, and began whacking my thighs. Instinctively, I threw one hand back and received a numbing blow on the elbow. A hand grabbed my neck, the fingernails cutting in. "Now, wise boy," he growled, "let me see you draw some blood!" I looked at the face across from me, a strong, good-looking face, but the eyes were like a furtive animal's.

"I . . . I can't," I stammered involuntarily.

"What? What?" My taskmaster was incredulous. "We'll see about that," There was a searing pain across my rear. As if that weren't enough, he began to kick me directly in the anus. I couldn't take it. I whirled. For an instant I had lost my senses and wanted nothing more from life than to kill him. My fighting spirit was short-lived, however. He battered me until I fell, groveling. "Next time, little bastard. . ." he puffed. "Next time I'll knock your damned head off." I was yanked to my feet. "Now do you still want to fight? All right . . . get back in line!"

My body was burning as the boy across from me urged, "Come on, hit me! Hit me, I can take it!" My knuckles met his cheek, hard.

"Harder!" the *hancho* shouted, and I kept striking, harder and harder.

Finally The Pig called a halt. "Now, recruits," he explained, "you are acquainted with *Taiko Binta*—a splendid game—*ha?* What, you don't think so? Well, you just need a little more practice. Then you can write home and tell your mothers what fun you've been having."

6

THE GRAND WAY OF HEAVEN AND EARTH

Afterward all of us lay sick, trying to smother our groans. About me men were vomiting. My head throbbed and the barrack seemed to rock like a ship. I lay on my side, trying to reflect on what had really happened, trying to comprehend why. It was no use—everything was utter pain and confusion.

40

All at once, I started. Someone had touched me. "Don't get excited," a voice whispered.

"What?" I blurted.

"Quiet! It is I—Nakamura." He was standing, a finger of light from outside cutting across his face and bare shoulders —taller than I and well-built, with a rather bad complexion.

"*Ah so!*" I responded. "The one who . . ." I turned on my side and massaged my bottom, not knowing what to say. He just stood there. "Well," I grunted, after a moment, "please sit down." As I shifted my legs the pain stabbed me then.

"Well . . ." he rubbed his own rear, "all right." Gingerly he lowered himself. "My behind still hurts from the first night. I just wanted to tell you . . . I'm sorry for hitting you so hard. Please be forgiving."

"Oh, that," I replied and tried to grin. "What is there to be sorry for? You couldn't help it. It's those filthy *hancho.*"

"Yes," he agreed, "those rotten bastards." After a silence he said, "You know, somebody's going to kill those bastards some day . . . every last one of them . . . kill them all . . . smash their rotten heads in."

"I hope so," I said. I waited, hoping he'd leave, for the pain was coming in waves and it took all my strength just to lie still. Finally the tension became unbearable and I tried to sit up. "Well"—I grunted the words—"I'm sorry that I had to hit you so hard. I hit you pretty hard, and I hope that you'll forgive me. I guess you know that I really hated to, I really didn't want . . ." Actually, I didn't care much what I said, or what I had done, not just then. Anything just to ease the pain, and the words fell out in a jumble.

But Nakamura just sat there, and inwardly I began to curse him. I closed my eyes, bit my lips, clenched and unclenched my hands. Why didn't he go? Couldn't he see what hell I was going through? He hadn't been hurt half as badly as I.

"You'd better not let the *shuban kashikan* find you up," I told him, and hated myself. We both knew that they wouldn't be back till morning.

"I know," he replied, but still remained, motionless. After a while I found that by tightening every muscle in my body, the pain would lessen. I worked out a little system, tightening my muscles, breathing several times, then relaxing as long as I could stand to. Doing this rhythmically, I began to feel better. I looked at the boy beside me, suddenly sensing how lonely he was. That was why he wouldn't leave!

41

"Where are you from?" I whispered.

"Kure," he answered, then confided: "You know, I always knew this would be rough, but I never thought anybody could be as rotten as these dirty . . . They're sadists, do you know that? Every single *hancho* is a sadist."

"Of course they are," I agreed. "How do you think they pick them? They go out, and look all around the country. Whenever they see someone whipping his mother, or maybe kicking his little sister in the head, they say, 'Come on, come on; we have a special job for you—*hancho* at Hiro Air Base.'"

"Yes, and besides that," Nakamura said, "every other one of them is queer."

"Not really?" I was ready to believe almost anything by now.

"Just wait," he warned me, "You'll find out. My brother's in the army. They gave him a rough time. It's not going to be any different here. He told me all about it."

"Really?" I was aghast at the idea. "My brother's in the army too, but he never told me anything about *that*."

"You'll be finding out soon enough. They're probably all perverts. That Pig, you can tell he's queer, just looking at him."

Deciding to change the subject, I said, "Do you think they have the tough training that we do—in the army, I mean?"

"I doubt it," he replied. "Maybe, though. Some of those forced marches they go on probably take a lot of guts—a lot of endurance and patience. They get beaten, too. I guess it's all about the same when it comes right down to it."

The pain had eased, now that I had concentrated on something else, and I wanted to sleep. I wondered how Nakamura could remain seated there so long. "Of course," he went on, "we don't have it as rough as those navy pilots. The men that make it through basic training in the navy air force— they're tough, believe me. There's hardly anything that can stop them."

"How could anybody have it rougher than we do?" I mumbled, and drifted into a dead sleep while he was still talking.

When I awakened it was six in the morning. I groaned, feeling, remembering. For a while it was impossible to imagine that I was really away from home. The others were stirring, and reveille had just sounded. The groans became general as the close-cropped heads emerged from the blankets. Yes, it was all real enough. For an instant I closed my eyes, as if such action might change conditions.

It was then, for a flickering instant, that a vision of home came—my own room all to myself, warmth, mother and Tomika. The homesickness flooded over me, and I began to cry inside. It was too cruel. Life just couldn't be so cruel. This couldn't be happening!

But it was happening. Sakigawa and Kakuda ("The Snake") were clumping through, cuffing the slow risers. They dumped a cot over, sprawling a recruit in a tangle of blankets. It was Nakamura.

I had to get up—fast! A spasm of fear hit me. I couldn't move! For several seconds my legs would bend no better than wood. My right arm throbbed at the elbow, and seemed completely paralyzed. With a wrench I rolled from my cot, the pain coming like glass splinters as I hit the floor. The shock brought life to my limbs, though, and I made it to my feet, hobbling and limping into my pants and shirt.

I laced my boots at a furious pace, but Sakigawa and The Snake, passing by, merely ordered, "Get a move on!"

Our beds made, we rushed to the first formation grunting and grimacing. As we fell in, staring rigidly ahead, I realized that every man had his share of welts and sores. Glancing from the corners of my eyes, I could see the swollen faces, cuts and bruises.

The Pig was all smiles as he surveyed us. "Stiff?" he asked. "Sore? Ah, what a pity." He pursed his thick lips. "But naturally, that's to be expected. You are all soft and flabby like old women. You're puny. You have no stamina. Japan's noble sons! Well, twenty minutes of running should help limber you up."

"Naturally, I would love to run along with you but, as you know, we *hancho* are sadly discriminated against." He cast his eyes downward long-sufferingly. "We are forced to ride bicycles."

Having formed us into a single column, he commanded, "Forward march!" Every step was torture. We were like broken old men. "Terrible! Terrible!" our *hancho* shouted. "Since you don't know how to walk, we shall try running. Double time, march!" Something cracked and the rear man blundered forward, crashing into the man ahead. Slowly, achingly, our column moved out, like a row of waddling ducks.

As we hobbled down the airstrip The Pig circled leisurely about on his bicycle, alternately screeching, cursing, cackling and cracking jokes, wielding a length of bamboo about an inch and a half in diameter. After we had double-timed for about half a mile, several of the men began to slow. "Faster, faster!" The Pig spurred them on.

Within a mile some of the men were falling behind. One man fell back a few feet, then a few yards, farther and farther. The Pig, up ahead, glanced back and wheeled about. As we reached the far end of the strip starting the turn, I looked back. The man was down, and The Pig was flailing him with the bamboo rod. But even this failed. The man had fainted.

As the grind continued, others dropped out. One stumbled, pitching to the concrete. Two comrades helped him to his feet, and his legs dangled pathetically as they bore him forward. It was impossible, of course, for them to keep up and shortly The Pig returned to flog all three of them. Having finished, he sped down the line thrashing at us. "This is how a fighter plane attacks!" he yelled. "Fast! Unexpected! Deadly!" He rolled along, bonking each man's head—"One, two, three, four, five, six . . ." Fortunately his aim wasn't always accurate.

I felt the blow glance off my head, and an instant later, intent on his role of fighter pilot, The Pig ran into one man, and pitched over with a wonderous crash. "You clumsy ass!" he squawked.

How I rejoiced! The glorious pilot has been shot down," I told myself.

As the run became more grueling, men began fainting one after another until there were only four or five of us left. Apparently The Pig had been scraped a bit, for he called a halt. All of us were panting and gasping, but I had to admit that a lot of the stiffness was gone. As we sagged, supposedly at attention, the "fighter pilot" scowled at us, then, smiling, remarked, "Nothing like a brisk walk before breakfast, boys —*ha*?" The bamboo stick was cracked, almost falling apart.

It was the start of a bad day. During our regular lunch hour, The Snake introduced us to more games, the last of which involved squirming along on our stomachs beneath our cots—around and around the barracks. This, because the floor was "dirtier than a pigpen." I dragged along watching the next man's heels kicking before me. The mere contact with the floor seemed to drug me, and I was overwhelmed with the urge to sleep. How wonderful, if I could quietly ease out of that serpentine procession—just to lie there beneath a cot after everyone else had gone—and sleep, sleep. The desire came in a whirling pool, but then a voice yelled, "Get moving over there!" I scrambled forward, ramming my face into the boots ahead of me.

After a while The Snake left, and the KP's brought our mess in the "honey buckets." Ravenously I attacked my bowl of rice, when someone said, "Hello, Kuwahara, old friend."

"Hello, Nakamura!" I said. "Please be seated." Nothing but a stereotyped greeting, and we were too hungry to talk much —but it was good to have a friend. Nakamura had been one of those who hadn't fallen out during our "brisk walk" in the morning.

"That dirty son of a bitch," Nakamura half-whispered. "Got some of his own medicine this morning, didn't he?"

"Yes," I agreed. "Came down right on his head."

Actually, neither of us had seen The Pig fall, but it was rather satisfying to suppose that he had lighted on his head. Before long several men, gleefully repeating the incident, said that our *hancho* had landed "right on his head."

"You wait," Nakamura assured me. "That fat ass will really get it one of these times. Some dark night. . ."

"He'll be getting it, all right," I concurred. Again, this was only wishful thinking, but it was enjoyable. Merely thinking such things, knowing that others were doing the same gave my spirit a lift. At first most of the boys had been reticent but, as brothers in misery, we rapidly grew friendly. To have someone to commiserate with, someone to hate with, was good.

Our brief respite ended, and soon we were learning more games. When we failed to perform our calisthenics acceptably we were forced to lie on our sides, then raise ourselves off the ground, balancing on one hand and foot, the opposite limbs extended skyward. An interesting experiment, and easily performed at first. But as the minutes passed, it grew more difficult. Eventually it became impossible to remain in that absurd position for more than a few seconds without collapsing. Time after time we balanced, making X's of our bodies, felt our arms and legs quiver, shake, and give way. Half an hour passed, and by then we thudded to the ground without even balancing.

45

And by this stage our *hancho* were beginning to use whips. We lay panting, moaning, awaiting the sting of a whip or the thud of a bat. Once the whip came like a splash of acid across my neck and ear, but I only cringed and tried to cover up. I was just about paralyzed.

During the day we were initiated into a dozen new forms of punishment, and that night at final formation the Pig brought activities to a fitting climax. We had failed to recite the five main points of the Imperial Oath, or Rescript, correctly.

I soon came to realize that improper performance in this regard brought severe chastisement more quickly than did any other infraction. The Imperial Rescript to Soldiers and Sailors, issued by the Emperor Meiji in 1882, is regarded as no less than sacred—a document several pages long, which every military man must learn verbatim. All are required to absorb its complex rules and philosophy through continual study and meditation. Every man must be prepared to recite it, complete or in part, at a moment's notice.

Sometimes Japanese fighting men were required to recite it in full at each night's formation, the chanting going on for about fifteen minutes. However, we at Hiro usually recited only the five main points or precepts:

(1) The soldier and sailor should consider loyalty their essential duty. . . . A soldier or a sailor in whom the spirit is not strong, however skilled in art or proficient in science, is a mere puppet; and a body of soldiers or sailors wanting in loyalty, however well-ordered and disciplined it may be, is in an emergency no better than a rabble. . . . With single heart fulfill your essential duty of loyalty, and bear in mind that duty is weightier than a mountain, while death is lighter than a feather. . . .

(2) Inferiors should regard the orders of their superiors as issuing directly from the Emperor. Always pay due respect not only to your superiors but also to your seniors, even though not serving under them. On the other hand, superiors should never treat their inferiors with contempt or arrogance. Except when official duty requires them to be strick and severe, superiors should treat their inferiors with consideration, making kindness their chief aim, so that all grades may unite in their service to the Emperor. . . .

(3) The soldier and the sailor should esteem valor. Ever since the ancient times valor has in our country been held

in high esteem, and without it our subjects would be unworthy of their name. How then may the soldier and the sailor, whose profession it is to confront the enemy in battle, forget even for one instant to be valiant? . . .

(4) Faithfulness and righteousness are the ordinary duties of a man, but the soldier and sailor, in particular, cannot be without them and remain in the ranks even for a day. Faithfulness implies the keeping of one's word and righteousness the fulfillment of one's duty. If then you wish to be faithful and righteous in anything, you must carefully consider at the outset whether you can accomplish it or not. If you thoughtlessly agree to do something that is vague in its nature, and bind yourself to unwise obligations, and then try to prove yourself faithful and righteous, you may find yourself in great straits from which there is no escape. . . .

(5) The soldier and the sailor should make simplicity their aim. If you do not make simplicity your aim, you will become effeminate and frivolous and acquire fondness for luxurious and extravagant ways; you will grow selfish and sordid and sink to the last degree of baseness, so that neither loyalty nor valor will avail to save you from the contempt of the world. . . . Never do you, soldiers and sailors, make light of this injunction.

These precepts are termed "The Grand Way of Heaven and Earth, the universal law of humanity," and men who have made a single mistake in their recitation have been known to kill themselves.

Thus it was understandable that The Pig laid such stress on this aspect of our training, for it was supposedly that very "soul of soldiers and sailors," and, of course, of our airmen. At the same time it seemed a bit paradoxical that he and his assistants should have such a strange way of complying with the injunction about treating inferiors with consideration.

That night, because of our negligence in failing to memorize precepts, we were lined up facing the barrack, and one by one our faces were slammed against the wall. One man received a broken nose, and another lost some teeth.

"Recruits," The Pig later informed us, "this has been an eventful day. A few more like this and you will become men!"

7

A TIME TO CRY

In one week my entire life had changed—my entire concept of man, of good and bad, of right and wrong. But it was impossible for me to evaluate my feelings at the time, any more than a severely wounded man might immediately interpret pain.

The initial shock had produced a numbness, a psychological paralysis. And emerging from it all was a continual dread. It was absolutely impossible to obey the injunction not to fear a superior. We became as furtive as rats that have suffered electric shock. It was impossible at first to find even one moment when we could relax. We were always crouched, awaiting the next shock.

For a time I actually believed that the life with my family, the carefree school days, had been nothing but a fond illusion. How far off they were now—and how vague. Time is a relative thing. The youth in me was being purged away. One week had made me old.

"*Shinpei, shinpei, kutsu migaki. Mata nete naku noka yo.*" These words have long been sung by Japanese recruits at *Shoto Rappa*, after the hard day. "Recruit, recruit, polish your shoes. Later you may cry in bed." The night has always been a time of sorrow for the trainee, a time when he can reminisce, take a deep breath, then under cover of darkness release his pent-up emotions, the pain and the fear.

After the *shuban kashikan* had completed their inspections, after any further disciplinary action, we lay in our cots thinking of home, especially of our mothers, sometimes our sisters. After all, some of us were only fifteen. Possibly we took a certain satisfaction in our very sorrow; people do at times. Lacking others to sympathize with us, we sympathized with ourselves. It was then that we shed our tears where no one could see and few would hear.

Some of the recruits, like me, had voices that were only beginning to change. In our dreams we sometimes called aloud for our mothers. Strangely, I never once heard a recruit call the name of his father. (Later I was to learn that dying men almost always ask for their mothers.) The father is the master of the family and it is partly his stern and rather remote love that helps instill a son with the fighting spirit. But when comfort is needed, or when a man has little time left upon the earth, then he thinks of his mother.

To one unfamiliar with the Japanese mind, some of our actions, our weeping and sentimentality, may appear surprising. To the outsider we are a poker-faced people who rarely register emotion. It is true that we have built up a certain façade. Ours is a philosophy of resignation in many ways, and frequently we display no feeling, even when filled with joy, or with hate. At times we may laugh at adversity. But all men share the same passions. They merely manifest them differently.

The Westerner, especially the American, I believe, may be compared to a boiling pot with a loose lid from which steam escapes regularly, without difficulty. The Japanese, on the other hand, is more like a pressure cooker. The same heat is applied and the same steam exists, but in the latter instance the steam may build up for a time without any outward manifestation. When at long last it does break forth, it may do so with violence.

Hence, it can better be comprehended how a Japanese in one instance can be the epitome of serenity, of gentle politeness, almost toadishness in his deference to others, and how at another time he may cast himself to the floor in hysterics— how also, he can attack his enemy with fanaticism.

Despite these considerations, however, every effort was made by our *hancho* to stifle all emotionalism, except as it pertained to country and emperor. Consequently, there was continual emphasis on channeling every emotion toward a greater cause. Ideally, every fear, anxiety, and joy was to be subdued, converted, and expressed in the mold of the fighting spirit. Therein all personal concern was subordinated. Whimpering because of pain or crying for one's mother were not only signs of weakness, they were indications that our lives were not yet dedicated to the Great Cause. Not yet had we learned the vital lesson that, as individuals, we were expendable—that the expenditure was no loss if it served a great enough end.

If a recruit moaned in his sleep and was overheard, we were all punished. At night we were often roused from bed, to be greeted by The Pig—in no mood for joking. The smirk would be gone, the face contorted—sometimes very weary.

"Can it be that you pitiful babies are soon to be honored sons of Japan, fighting for the glory of our esteemed emperror?" Shaking his head: "I am here to make men of you, and I refuse to be a failure! Do you understand? I'll make a man of every recruit here, even if I have to kill him. It fills us with trepidation to think that our emperor has deigned, has even considered, to honor such miserable excuses for manhood.

"Now, *shinpei*, I am going to give some friendly advice—especially to those who bawl every night like snot-nosed kids. You are here for one reason. Do you know what that reason is? Do you?" When we had chorused our reply, he would sneer. "No you don't; it's obvious. You exist for only one reason—for your emperor and for Nihon, your country."

Very gently he would say, "I suggest that you forget about the past altogether. There is no past. Get that into your heads once and forever. There is only the present." Growing more emphatic again, gesticulating, he would continue: "Forget about the past! Forget about civilian life! Forget about your families! From now on you live for only one purpose. You will be prepared to die at a moment's notice without flinching. Never, never forget that you are Japan's most expendable item. The sooner you accept this fact, the better off you'll be!"

More softly again: "Now . . . the *binta*, the ball bats, the other things . . . they are nothing, nothing at all. But they make men of you—prepare you for greater tests. Do you understand now? Good!" He motioned to The Snake and Sakigawa. "Bring the bats!"

Most of us were beaten unconscious, and we didn't make a sound.

How strange that punishment was! Although the majority of us were very young, there were a few recruits anywhere from forty-five to sixty years old. And those men were treated with no more consideration than anyone else. The military was an enormous melting pot, where each man lost his identity. Every man's head was cropped. Every man wore the same uniform. Elderly, rich, people of prestige—all were the same. The *hancho* who would have bowed in obeisance to some of the trainees in civilian life, or who might not even have been able to associate with them, was a tyrant and ruler over all. He could kick or strike any recruit with impunity.

After the first week had passed at Hiro, we began sleeping

as though we were drugged. Our bodies had not yet become conditioned to either the punishment or the arduous training routine. Sometimes during the night as we lay almost in a coma, The Snake and Sakigawa, along with some of their cohorts, would enter the barracks to perform certain quaint tricks. Occasionally they would stealthily tie our hands and feet, then flash on the lights and order us to get up. In our stupor we would struggle to arise, often tumbling to the floor in bewilderment. It usually took a while for us to realize what had happened, and the *hancho* always laughed uproariously at our frantic efforts to get untied.

When Nakamura had first declared that some of the *hancho* were perverted, I'd been startled and incredulous. As time went by, however, I began to think that perhaps he was right. While none of the *hancho* ever proved to be an outright homosexual, so far as I knew, more than one of them subjected us to embarrassment in various unsavory ways.

The Snake, more than anyone else, enjoyed humiliating the younger recruits before the others. Those of us who had barely attained puberty suffered the most. During a formation he might leer at some unfortunate who had just made a mistake, and say, "Hey, *shinpei,* you must still be a kid—na? Hey, *shinpei,* you a man yet? Didn't you hear right? I said, are you a man yet?"

"Yes, honorable *hancho-dono,*" the reply always came.

"*Ah so!* Prove it, *shinpei!* Take down your pants! Now your *fundoshi!* Quick!"

Then the hapless trainee would stand shamefaced while The Snake, sometimes Sakigawa, or even The Pig, poked fun and made snide comments regarding his scant endowments. Such things I dreaded more than the physical punishment.

Late one night three of us were rousted from bed to clean the *hancho* quarters, because our work there during the day had been unsatisfactory. After we had finished the job we were forced to strip down and jump into the icy showers. As if this was not enough, The Snake then herded us out naked into the cold and had us run around the barracks five times. We were then locked in the shower room for the rest of the night, still without clothing.

There for the first hour we huddled on a wooden bench, cramped, cold—no lights. As the time dragged on, we decided to exercise. It was the only way to keep from growing numb. Once I awoke from a half-sleep and began doing push-ups,

51

feeling the cold from the cement floor knifing up through my hands and toes. In the midst of those exertions I suddenly thought of the showers. A flash of optimism. But it died. So far as I knew, the hot water was turned on only at intervals during the day.

Eventually, however, mainly for something to do, I groped my way over and twisted one of the handles. A sudden whoosh of cold, and I jerked back. As I reached out once more, to turn it off, the water felt tepid. It was growing warm!

Seconds later it was coming hot, steaming hot. Quickly I turned it off, and peered about furtively. Had the *hancho* heard the noise from their rooms? No, not through two doors, and they would be sound asleep by now. I glanced through the gloom at my companions, just their vague outlines. Squatting on the bench, back to back, they had managed to doze. For a moment I battled with myself. If I alone were to use the shower, the hot water might last for a long time. If all three of us used the showers . . .

But, after a moment I whispered, "Oka! Yamamoto! Hey, come over to the showers."

"Hot water?" Oka blurted.

"Quiet!"

In an instant the two were next to me, rubbing their arms and stomachs, hunching over, treading up and down. "Turn them on, quick!" Yamamoto groaned through clattering teeth.

"Just one," I said. "We won't turn it on too high, or all the water will be gone before we can even get warm." Obediently they stood back while I regulated the shower. Then we crowded beneath it, exclaiming as the water warmed our clammy flesh.

"Ah, this is great. This is wonderful!" I murmured, tilting my head back. Then another idea struck me. "I wonder if . . .? Where's something to stop up the drain?"

"Sit on it," Oka replied gleefully. "Your ass is big enough."

It might be possible, I decided, to fill the small shower room three or four inches deep without flooding the rest of the floor. Suddenly I knew what to use—toilet paper! And the plan worked perfectly. I covered the drain with a layer about half an inch thick, and the water gradually covered the floor around us, soaking through just fast enough to prevent the outer room from flooding.

"Why don't you both admit I'm a genius?" I said, and settled back in the gurgling liquid. Eventually the shower had created enough steam to warm the atmosphere around us. I stretched supine in the deepening water. That wa mth—it was wonderful. There in the midst of the cold, the dark, and the cruelty, we had found our own secret little island.

And in this warm seclusion I fell asleep.

8

THE COST OF SUSHI CAKES

Despite the constant reminders to forget the past, after two weeks our families were permitted to pay us a brief visit. Only fourteen days since I had said *sayonara*, and it seemed ages. As the hour approached for the visit I began to tremble. It had been so very long! So much had happened. Home seemed a thousand miles away.

It was 4:00 P.M. I waited in the visiting room where a counter separated the trainees, as if they were convicts, from their families. I watched different families enter, observed how each trainee's eyes lit in recognition. Some of them seemed almost embarrassed, hesitant. The bar hampered them from making any intimate greeting, and the best they could do was clasp hands.

Thirty minutes passed. Still my family hadn't appeared. I began to fidget. Didn't they realize that we had only a brief hour together? They might not arrive until too late. It would serve them right.

Then again, they might not come at all. They had misunderstood the visiting date, that was it. I must have written it down wrong in my letter. I cracked my knuckles, and stared at the floor.

Then I glanced toward the door. There was father in his gray business suit, its conservative shade blending with the two drab *monpei* (wartime *kimono*) behind him. Mother and Tomika. Soon we were clasping hands, looking into each other's eyes. Mother and Tomika made no effort to disguise their feelings, beaming through watering eyes. I couldn't speak, and it was tough fighting my own tears back. But I bit my lip, determined to show no weakness before my father.

53

Father's smile had never been quite so warm: "How is your new life, my son?"

"Oh . . ." I faltered. "It is fine, father." At that moment something writhed inside me and the words in my mind pounded: "Why do you lie? Tell the truth! Tell of the cruelty, the injustice! Tell him that you want to leave. Maybe he can do something. . . ."

But then, father had been in the army. Surely he knew what I was going through. He'd been through about the same thing. How had he managed to survive so well? He squinted one eye and raised the opposite brow. "Do your *hancho* love you? Are they kind and gentle, like your mother? You are looking fine. I believe your face has filled out from all the good food." Truly, my face had filled out—swollen from the previous night's *binta*.

"It's not from . . ." I began, then stopped. Father's dark eyes held mine. His head gave a quick little shake. "Are they treating you well, Yasuo?" he persisted.

I smiled. "Yes, thank you, father—quite well."

For a little while none of us spoke. Then Tomika bent forward, her brow wrinkled, looking into my face as if it were a mirror. "How did you get those cuts?"

"Yasuo-*chan*, your eyes are black! You've been hurt!" Mother's voice carried that tone of concern I was so familiar with. A struggle began within me. The child part of me found comfort, yet I felt a strange irritation. "They've been cruel to you! Absolutely cruel!" She spoke so loudly I flushed and glanced at the people nearest us. But they were all absorbed in their own conversations. "Yasuo-*chan* . . ." she said, almost pleadingly, as though there were anything I could do to change it.

"It is nothing, mother, nothing at all!" I answered bruskly.

"But Yasuo-*chan* . . . your poor, dear eye . . ."

"It is nothing, mother! It is nothing at all!" I fairly shouted. "I just fell down. It will be better in no time!" Then I had to hold my hand over my eyes as though shading them from the sun. There was a silence while I breathed jerkily. All the while mother's hand pressed mine. Right then I loved my mother more than I ever had—more than anything that ever was or would be.

Quietly father said, "My son can take care of himself. Already he has become a man. He is a *samurai!*" I looked up, rubbing my face with my fist, and smiled.

54

"Your sister and I have made some *sushi* cakes," mother said. Will they permit you to have them?" Both mother and Tomika had concealed food under the cloth *obi* about their waists. Their *sushi* cakes had long been a favorite with me.

"We're not supposed to," I said, "but they'll never know anything about it—if you can just hand it to me without anyone's seeing. Did you bring the shirts and towels?" Mother nodded and placed a square bundle on the counter, tied in a orange *furoshiki*. "Just slip the cakes inside," I suggested. "No one will ever find out."

Ironically, almost the moment after she had passed the bundle to me there was a commotion. The *hancho* was cuffing one of the trainees, while his entire family watched in consternation. "Beat me! Beat me!" his mother wailed. "It isn't my son's fault! It is my fault. He didn't ask me to bring him anything." The cuffing wasn't severe, but it was mortifying to all of us. Sunday was the one day in the week when we were supposed to receive decent treatment. This was to have been our brief interlude, a fleeting moment when everything could be serene. The *hancho* himself was not more than eighteen or nineteen—with a long neck and a shiny, arrogant face. He could easily have punished the recruit later. How I would have loved to kill him.

Realizing what had happened, mother became frantic and urged me to return the food before anything could happen. I wavered for an instant, and then rebellion filled me. "No! Those . . . You and Tomika made it for me, and I'm going to keep it."

Tomika murmured, and their eyes looked haunted. "Let him have his *sushi*," father said. "They can't hurt a Kuwahara. Let him keep it."

The matter was settled. Soon the visiting hour was over, and the women were again tearful. "Stop it!" father ordered. "Do you think a man likes to see tears all the time?" He reached over and clasped my arms firmly. "We shall see you in a short while, when your basic training is over, *na?*"

I nodded. "We get a leave."

"All right," he said, "it won't be long, and you'll enjoy it. Learn all you can, and come to us a true *samurai*. Make us proud of you, Yasuo." I nodded again, and they were leaving. Father strode out the door without looking back. Tomika turned once, her large eyes like a fawn's. I waved uncertainly, and they were gone.

Later in the barrack, most of the men lay on their cots, a privilege we were accorded only on Sunday, and stared at the ceiling. The visit hadn't elevated our spirits very much. I saw Nakamura hunched on the edge of his cot, his chin in his hands. Strolling over, I stood eying him, but he said nothing. Thinking I shouldn't bother him, I paced slowly about the room, kicking at the floor. Then I stopped by his cot again. *"Yai,* Nakamura! You like *sushi* cakes?"

Grinning faintly he glanced up. "Have you got some too?"

"Un," I said, "hidden under my blankets."

Nakamura laughed and patted his own bedding. "Me too!"

Before long we discovered that nearly everyone had received one kind of food or another—cake, candy, or cookies. Oka and Yamamoto had their shirts stuffed, and were busily hiding their contraband. "We'll have a party!" Oka exclaimed. "Tonight after *Shoto Rappa!"* The thought filled us with glee, and we laughed heartily for the first time in two weeks.

Unfortunately our happy interlude was short-lived. Upon returning from evening chow, held in the mess hall on Sundays, we found that our beds had been ransacked. Several of us were whispering excitely when The Pig made his entry. "Oh!" Someone exclaimed involuntarily.

"Oh?" The Pig said. "What do you mean, 'Oh'?" In a most disarming manner, he laid a hand on Oka's shoulder. "Is something missing?"

Oka stiffened. "No, honorable *hancho-dono."*

"Well, what's the matter then? Why did you say, 'Oh'?" Oka faltered incoherently. "Are you men sure that nothing is amiss?" The Pig queried. "I sense a restraint. What can be wrong?"

"Nothing is wrong, honorable *hancho-dono,"* Nakamura bravely volunteered.

"Hmmm," The Pig stroked his jaw, and strolled back and forth for a full minute, fully enjoying the situation. "Could it be that I am not wanted?" Suddenly, without the slightest warning, he whirled, jabbing a finger at Yamamoto: "Why is your bed torn up?" Yamamoto gagged. "Very curious," The Pig muttered, and struck a stance, one hand on his hip, the other stroking his jaw again. "My, this is a weird situation. I come in here, hoping for a little friendship, and what do I get? Not one kind word, only coldness. I ask a decent question and hardly anyone will even speak to me."

The Pig flounced down on my cot, nearly collapsing it. The

actor was coming out in him, as it was so often wont to. "Look at me, Kuwahara." He buried his face in his hands and made blubbering noises. Looking up with a stricken expression he lamented, "Kuwahara, what can this all mean?"

"I, I don't know, honorable—"

"I'm a stranger in my own family! Children! My children, don't you even remember your mother?" He went back to his weeping.

An excellent performance, and it was difficult to keep from laughing, even though we realized it all presaged something unpleasant.

At last The Pig tired of his game, and informed us in a rather bored manner that we would have to be chastised for attempting to trick him. We were herded outside and our faces were slammed against the barracks. But this was only the beginning. Later we were forced to crawl about the barrack with our combat boots tied about our necks. In this manner we traveled down the halls to visit the *hancho* in their various rooms. It was something like an initiation ceremony, I suppose. Each man, in turn, knocked on a closed door. Upon being granted admittance, he entered on hands and knees to apologize.

When I entered The Pig's quarters he was seated under a bright light, for special effect, legs crossed and an arm hooked over the back of his chair. Sighing and blowing a jet of cigar smoke at me, he remarked, "Aren't you well enough fed here?"

"Yes, honorable—"

"Then why did you bring food into your quarters when you knew perfectly well that it was forbidden?"

"I am sorry, honorable *hancho-dono.*"

"Well, Kuwahara—look at me, not at the floor—I'm afraid that sorry is not enough." All the while he kept blowing billows of rancid cigar smoke into my face. When I began to gag from the effects he said, "What in the world's the matter with you? Are you ill? Do I disgust you?" Before I could reply he continued, "As I was saying, Kuwahara, we wouldn't accomplish much at this base—as a matter of fact, we'd lose the war—if every man could break the rules, and then just say 'I'm sorry.' No indeed! I fear I shall have to chastise you for your deception. Besides, I resent not being invited to the little party you were planning after *Shoto Rappa.* I was a recruit once, you know."

He then kicked me in the face, and called blandly, "Next, please!"

"Thank you for your trouble, honorable *hancho-dono*," I mumbled, and crawled for the door, my boots swinging.

9

THE PARTING OF MIYAGAME

Severe as it was, our punishment of the first few weeks was negligible compared to what came later. As we hardened, they began running us five miles each day instead of two or three. Eventually we were running over eight miles, and those who fell behind were bludgeoned with rifle butts.

During the *binta*, instead of exchanging fist blows in the face, we used shoes with hob nails in them, and there was not one man whose face was not ripped, especially around the corners of the mouth. Except for Sundays, the torment was incessant.

It was toward the end of the first month that the men really began to break. Continual pain, continual humiliation, continual pressure. It could not be endured forever. The two remaining months of basic loomed like centuries. I didn't believe it possible that all of us could last out the time. And I was right.

Six men from our original group deserted. They scaled the barbed-wire enclosure, only to be captured a short time later. One of them remained free for several days, hiding in mountains, stealing vegetables from the farms by night. He was caught finally by civilian police near his home in Hongo City. In order to verify that he was actually an escapee the police delivered him to his family. What ignominy! "We are sorry," the police said, "but this man has betrayed his country, and we have no recourse but to return him to Hiro." Then he was led away, handcuffed.

It was standard procedure that deserters from all branches of the military were sent to army stockades, where they were completely at the mercy of the vicious MP's. Reports had reached us that prisoners were often tortured to death in the stockades, with no recourse to justice. The authorities in the stockades fabricated various reasons for the demise of men in such cases, and were rarely questioned.

Many of the recaptured deserters were hung from the ceiling by their wrists with iron weights attached to their ankles. Their naked backs were beaten with belts.

For all of us, time moved by like an inchworm, but those of us who didn't completely break under the ordeal were gradually toughening—in mind and body. Somehow we made it through the gristmill of the second month. Two-thirds of it was behind us now. "You've made it for two whole months," I kept telling myself! "surely you can last just one more!"

During the weeks at Hiro I had grown noticeably and was grimly satisfied that I could stand hardship as well as the next man—a lot better than most. In calisthenics and in endurance running I was one of the top men. I continued to excel at glider practice, as well as in the various training classes. My championship title became known to many of my companions, without my ever having said much about it. And this, I suppose, gave me a certain prestige.

My general outlook was truly improving when a shock came—one which demoralized me for days.

One evening I finished polishing my boots and strolled to the latrine. As I approached the door, a recruit informed me that it was locked. "Out of order, I guess," he said, and wandered off.

Feeling an urgent need to enter, however, I waited a minute and tried the knob. "Anybody in there?" I called. It occurred to me that possibly The Snake had locked the door from the outside, just to cause us some discomfort. It was the sort of trick he might have done.

The latch was a flimsy one, and my need to get inside was growing. After glancing about to see whether anyone was watching, I reared back on one leg and crashed my heavy boot heel against the lock. The lock creaked and the door shuddered. Once again I glanced around, then assaulted the lock with greater determination. This time it gave, and the door fell open.

Not wishing to be found out, I entered hastily, leaving the light off. It was then that I collided with somone . . . something. "What is . . . Pardon me," I mumbled. No answer. Something, a presence, seemed to loom before me in the dark. Backing toward the door, I blurted, "What's wrong?" Someone was there. I'd touched someone. He was just standing there, like a madman. Dark, the stench, and silence—all mingled in one.

I groped for the wall switch, flipped it. . . . Light revealed the limp figure, dangling from a rafter—still swinging from our contact.

This was my first close acquaintance with death. It was Miyagame, a fellow I had talked with more than once. I remembered now . . . quiet and withdrawn . . . always rather wan and frail. Miyagame! He was the one the *hancho* had slapped, before his family, on visitors' day.

Back and forth, back and forth. He just kept swinging. I stared in horrid fascination. It was only a moment that I stood there as if in a dream, but it seemed a long time before panic gripped me—suddenly aware that there still might be life somewhere within that gray flesh—fearing that the last drops might be ebbing even as I watched. I started toward him, then turned and rushed into one of the billets. "Quick! Let me take your bayonet!" I said to a startled recruit.

"Nani? What is it?" He blinked at me stupidly.

Seizing the bayonet atop his locker, I shouted, "There's a man in the latrine—a dead man! Hanged!" The recruit rose slowly, looking as if he'd just bitten into a wormy apple. "Come on!" I ordered. "Help me, for God's sake!" Dumbly he followed. I had a quick impression that he thought I was mad.

Then he saw Miyagame. I held the limp form and lowered it to the floor, as he cut the rope. Feverishly I began to apply artificial respiration. Whether it was five minutes or twenty, I don't know. I stopped when a voice said, "You're wasting your time, Kuwahara; he's dead." It was The Snake, and a dozen men were clustered around us.

Almost inaudibly someone said, "Anyway, he is happy now."

Swiftly the news spread, and the following day a letter was found, addressed to his family, a written apology for dishonoring them, asking their forgiveness also for "dying ahead of you before it was my rightful time." His final words read, "I await you in Heaven."

This was the real breaking point for many of our group. Now was the time when only the fittest would survive. Miyagame's suicide had created a terrible psychological effect.

My own special glow of hope and strength deserted me. What good would it do me to grow strong? After basic, there would be more punishment—more and more and more. Then what? Then I would die for an emperor who wouldn't even know about it, who would never even hear my name.

My visions of becoming a hero soured, rotted away. In their place was the bloated face of Miyagame, swinging, always swinging. Pictures started coming—Miyagame being slapped before his family, all of them burning with shame, and always after that, the latrine and the body. After *Shoto Rappa* I would close my eyes tight to force out what I knew must come. But always the swirl of thoughts would subside, leaving the gloom of the latrine, and Miyagame.

Swinging! He was always swinging! Tossing, clutching my pillow, I would clamp my eyes shut, only to lock the vision in tighter.

Steadily the daily punishment increased, but I dreaded the nights with Miyagame more than the days with the *hancho*. More than once I yelled in the night, and bolted upright, peering wildly into the dark. Each time my body was filmed with sweat—which I wiped away with a towel.

Finally the specific picture of Miyagame began to fade, only because other men had decided to follow him. Watanabe, another from my own quarters, went next, then two of the trainees that had entered Hiro shortly ahead of us, and still another of those who had entered just after. They died with ropes, bayonets, and one leaped off a building. Nine men committed suicide at Hiro during my basic training.

Suicide! It was a way out. Could it hurt any more to hang than to be bludgeoned with a rifle butt? Could it hurt any more to hang than to hug a tree naked, to cling to the rough, icy bark while your back was whipped? I found myself planning. Slashed wrists would probably be the best way. Yes, what would be simpler. That would be nothing compared to even the mildest punishment we were used to.

But each day I would feel my body toughening, feel the strength growing in my legs as we ran, and I would hear my father's voice calmly telling me to return a man, a *samurai*. Of course, I couldn't dishonor my father, not my family, not the name of Kuwahara. Only two more weeks of basic. Spring was coming. The sun was splashing on us as we ran around the strip. I could run forever. I could keep right on going through life the same way. They wouldn't stop me now!

Another week passed. The punishment reached an all-time high, but the fittest had survived. We were near the end, and the friendships were growing. Nakamura was like a brother, frank, sometimes outspoken, but understanding and courageous. I admired him. Yamamoto and Oka always lifted my spirits. Those two could laugh no matter what the situation. *Gokudo*— irresponsible pranksters, both of them—extroverts with plenty of grit.

Strangely enough, some of our punishment even became laughable. Occasionally, when the *hancho* were in an especially good mood, they would put us through a ludicrous routine. One of Sakigawa's favorite pastimes was to have a recruit climb atop a wall locker where he would squat, legs crossed, arms folded, much like a meditative Buddha. He was required to maintain this position, while the *hancho* shook the locker violently, jarring and teetering it. Eventually the recruit would tumble to the floor. Anyone not agile enough by this time to light without getting hurt wasn't worth much.

Occasionally we were ordered to climb trees just outside the barrack. We then had to roost there for ten or fifteen minutes, making humming sounds like a cicada. This was not only amusing to *hancho,* but to the rest of us as well. I remember Oka laughing almost hysterically, and slapping his leg while Yamamoto hummed down through the branches at us.

"Ah so!" The Snake had growled, cuffing Oka. "If it's that good, maybe you'd better try it yourself." Oka went up the trunk like a squirrel, perched near Yamamoto, wildly trying to out-hum him. It was hilarious, and every man that laughed was ordered up the tree. Soon the branches were clustered with recruits—together emitting the weirdest sound I have ever heard.

Toward the last, the punishment began to lessen. The commanding officer wanted us to look good when we returned home on leave. The *hancho* became almost human during the last few days. And The Pig, whom many of us had sworn to kill, invited the men from the most outstanding barrack to his home in Kure for a *sukiyaki* party.

It was a strange reversal. The man whom we had most dreaded, the man who had been largely responsible for the suicide of nine trainees, was now honoring us in his very home. We were respected guests!

The Pig's wife was surprisingly lovely—a perfect hostess— and his two children, a boy and girl, ages five and seven, were charming. For nearly two hours we sat, while Noguchi's wife filled our bowls time and again with food. It was amazing. All during that time The Pig chatted pleasantly, occasionally cracking jokes. Vainly I strove to understand the new role. For once he seemed completely genuine. In none of his conversation could I detect the faintest sarcasm, or a sinister nuance.

When he spoke of the punishment, he addressed us as if we were merely onlookers who had never experienced a trace of it. Wiping his mouth carefully and sipping his *sake,* he confided, "It does seem unfortunate that the men must be punished so severely at times. However. . ." He sighed with what seemed to be honest regret. "I have no recourse but to obey our commanding officer, and he, in turn, must obey those above him, and so it goes. The *Daihonei* becomes unhappy with the commanding officer of Hiro. He is chastised. The commanding officer becomes displeased with the officers under him. He chastises them. They chastise their *hancho.* The *hancho* chastise their trainees. Their trainees . . . they go home on leave and kick the dog." We laughed in unison.

"Of course punishment is important. It is absolutely necessary. Sad to admit, none of us is a born *samurai.* Don't be shocked. You learn to be a *samurai* by surviving rough treatment. Look at my *shinpei.* Are they tough? Yes, they are tough! They are not the same ones who thought I was killing them that first night three months ago.

"Yes, they hate *Hancho* Noguchi. They want to kill *Hancho* Noguchi. But they are better than the enemy now. It will take more to stop them, more to scare them, more to kill them. Some day soon they will know this is true. Then maybe Noguchi won't seem so bad." The Pig was accepting us as friends, confiding in us. He was talking about other men, not us. The suffering was remote, and yet it was understandable, more than it had ever been before.

The Pig had a purpose in inviting us to dinner. He had something to leave with us, for us to understand. We would pass it on to our friends.

Aside from this brief conversation, he spoke no more of the training. Instead he spoke to us of philosophy, poetry and art. His home was filled with books, and The Pig expatiated on a variety of subjects, astonishing us with his wisdom. Later his wife graciously played the *shamisen* and sang hauntingly, enchantingly. She sang the popular *Kojo-no-tsuki* and then a very old song. In the dimly lit room the flowers on her kimono seemed to glow, and the shadows on her smooth skin had turned to a quiet green. Half-closing my lids, I watched the curve of her cheek, the delicate nostrils, how the brow disappeared into the ebony of her hair. By squinting even more I could make her hair disappear, leaving just the face, the lips moving, the line of her neck.

From the corners of my eyes I observed the men around me. They were spellbound. I watched the woman's delicate fingers moving over the strings of the *shamisen*. I closed my eyes and wished. By wishing, I could obliterate everyone else. The Pig, my friends would all be gone. I would be alone with her, and I would sit close, looking into those liquid eyes. And when the songs were over she would slowly look at me, and her lips would arch. Her hands would reach out across the *shamisen* to touch my own.

The music was over too soon. We were bowing to The Pig, thanking him profusely. His wife in turn was bowing to us, laughing in the shrill notes of a little girl, notes that were at the same time ripe and womanly. Her laughter was not the result of amusement, merely a form of politeness. She acknowledged each of us with a bow as we filed out—each of us exactly the same. No, she wasn't even aware of how close I had sat beside her, or how she had touched me, the moment all the others were gone.

10

BRIEF REUNION

At long last basic training had ended. I had done it! I had come through! They had never broken me, and I was proud. Their psychology was sound. During the last few days the punishment had lessened, and we had become more comradely with the *hancho*. The commanding officer had assembled us the morning before our leave, speaking of our future obligations, informing us that now we were, indeed, men. We had been drilled daily in hand-to-hand combat, we were hard, we could withstand pain, we had seen death. Those who died had served a good purpose, toughening the rest of us, helping us to realize that the weakest are always the most expendable.

When we had assembled on the last day, a light mist was still lacing the base, and as the commanding officer spoke, it dispersed, revealing the rising sun. The rising sun! It was an omen. Our commander was a small man, like a finely honed razor, but his bearing bespoke power. Each gesture was emphatic and impressive.

I watched the sun flood about him, lighting the eagle insignias above his visor and on his lapels. When he had finished speaking, fifty basic trainees chanted the entire Imperial Rescript without a flaw. As the words poured forth I could hear the throb of planes in the distance—the two sounds merging, symbolizing our new-found power. I was a part of something great, something tremendous. Then, in the sun, I knew that the Imperial Way would encompass the world.

And now, the return to Onomichi on a two day leave before flying school. My family was there to meet me at the station, eager to usher me home. "Toshifumi is coming especially to see you!" Tomika babbled excitedly. "Toshifumi!" I exclaimed. "All the way from Tokyo—just to see me?"

"Well, perhaps your brother will at least say hello to the rest of us," father said, and we laughed together. Suddenly life was too good to be real. Two whole days with my family, my relatives, my friends. And I would not be returning to Hiro as a green *shinpei*.

Our home had never looked more beautiful. It was May, and the garden walls were festooned with azaleas. The mountains and fields were green.

First of all I wanted to take a hot bath, and lie back with the water up to my neck. Moments after entering the house I was seated on a small stool in the *yudono*, the bathing room, vigorously soaping. "Brother," Tomika's voice tinkled, "do you want your back washed?"

"Un!" I responded. It seemed more fitting than ever that a woman should wash my back now; I was a man. I hunched over slightly and hugged my knees as she entered, exposing only my rounded back. What occurred next was totally unexpected.

65

"Yasuo, what have they done to your back?" Tomika cried. I had forgotten about the many lash marks, but it was good to have her make something of the matter. "Oh, that's nothing. Those are just reminders of a little game we learned."

But my wounds were not to be passed off so easily, and I had hardly anticipated their effect upon Tomika. Concern—certainly. But my sister softly traced her fingers over the wounds, then burst into tears. "My own baby brother!" she wept.

"Tomika, I'm all right. It's all right! Those little things are nothing. They don't even bother me. I hardly even flinched when they gave them to me!" The wrong words, those last, for her wails increased. Tears flooding down her face, she stumbled into the alcove and cast herself on the *tatami* matting, wailing piteously about her little brother.

Hearing the commotion, mother hastened in. Tomika was inarticulate. "It's nothing, mother!" I said. "She just saw some little sores on my back." Mother cautioned Tomika to be silent, peered in at me, then entered and gently began soaping my back. With the wooden dipper she scooped water from the steaming bath, and sluiced it over me. *"Atsui?* Hot?" she inquired.

Truly, it was hot! *"Sukoshi,"* I said, "a little." There was no quick way of cooling the sunken bath, and since father always kept it on the verge of boiling, mother laid a scented towel across my back, and poured water through it.

As she turned to go, I noticed tears in her own eyes. *"Arigato,"* I thanked her, but she hastened out with no reply.

Cleansed and rinsed, I eased into the waiting caldron. I dipped one foot, let it cook a little, then slid my leg in. Clinging to the sides, I slowly lowered myself, breathed in sharply through my teeth as the water hit my scarred back, grunted and sank back. The pain ebbed and the heat grew more soothing, blissfully so. Not in three months had I been so relaxed, not even on that cold night in the shower with Oka and Yamamoto.

So many things I wanted to do during this leave, but now the bath was a drug. It seemed to assuage the pain of three long months, but it focused their weariness. Weakly I left the water, dried, donned my *yukata* and slippers, and shuffled up the stairs to my room. For a moment I gazed from my window at the mountains. A cooling breeze played across my face and chest. My eyes half-closed. The mountains faded. I was barely able to crawl beneath the *futon,* barely able to feel its softness. Irresistible sleep enfolded me.

When I revived, the sun was beginning its descent, lighting the room with amber. For a while I lay blinking, not sure where I was. Then I heard a door glide partly open on its rollers. No mistaking Tomika's whispers—but who else was with her? I bolted upright. "Toshifumi!" I cried. "Well have you come! All the way from Tokyo!"

Squatting beside me, he roughed my head. "Hello, *bozu,"* he smiled, referring to my hair that was cropped like a monk's. "Well, you've changed! You're almost a man!"

That last hurt, but I beamed back. Toshifumi again, after two whole years! He was not the same person who had so often grappled and cavorted with our brother, Shigeru, before the war. Now, dignified and handsome, he was surprisingly like father. There was even a faint white streak in his hair —rare for a Japanese his age.

After a brief visit he went downstairs, leaving me to dress. An hour or two later my uncle and aunt from Innoshima came to visit. Yes, my return was quite an event. Despite the growing scarcity of food, mother and Tomika had prepared a feast with all the delicacies I loved.

How touch I was by their devotion. By 1944, food was heavily rationed, and even good rice was hard to obtain. Mother and Tomika had walked several miles into the country the day before my return to obtain whole rice, polished, from a farmer—a precious commodity, which he would not have given up for mere money. Instead, Tomika had given him one of the beautiful and costly *kimono,* which was to have been part of her dowry. Then they had trudged home, carrying the bags of rice on their backs.

Truly an act of love, and I thanked them sincerely. When I mentioned Tomika's sacrifice, during the meal, she smiled and replied, "It was nothing. Anyway, by the time a man takes me for his wife, I will have accumulated a hundred *kimono."*

"Oh, come now!" Toshifumi chuckled, "There are plenty of men who would be elated to have you. Just wait!"

Tomika smiled, but there was a wistfulness in the way her glanced fled to her lap. "I'm twenty-six years old," she said simply.

"Tomika shall have a husband in due course," father announced, "when we find one worthy—one of proper station. I refuse to consider that fawning—ah, what's his name?"

"Must you humiliate your daughter before her relatives?" mother chided. Tomika arose, hiding her burning face, making quick little steps toward the door.

"Come back here!" father ordered. "Don't be so touchy!"

After a moment Tomika returned and sat staring meekly at the floor.

"Where is Reiko?" I asked.

"We . . . we had to let her go," mother answered. She smiled at my aunt and uncle. "The maid was actually just an unnecessary expense. Well, I mean it just seemed foolish, with a war on, and just the three of us at home now."

"Yasuo," my uncle suggested, "let us hear something of your experiences. How did you like your training?" Until evening we talked, of my training, of Toshifumi's dentistry, but mainly we listened as father and his brother recounted their own experiences in the army.

That night, after my relatives had departed, I was visited by Tatsuno. During our three months' separation Tatsuno had written me two letters, neither of which I had answered. Of course, I hadn't been given much spare time, but certainly I could have sent him a note. Somehow, each time I had started to write him, something had stopped me. Hiro wasn't something I wanted Tatsuno to experience.

But he was soon to be there, and would have gone a month sooner had he not torn the ligaments in his arm during a glider accident at school. There was something about Tatsuno so sensitive and keen that it hurt me to think of all he would soon be going through. He seemed too much like Miyagame, who had found a way out by hanging.

Because of this, and because I was now a man with some military experience behind me, I gave Tatsuno much advice. "It will be tough," I said, "but remember that the first two months are the hardest; remember not to flinch the first time they hit you with the ball bat. . . . Don't ever show any disrespect for your *hancho*. . . . Don't ever do anything that would attract special attention to you; just be one of the group. . . . How's your endurance? Can you double-time at least three miles? Well, you'd better start getting in shape these last few days before you go in. Then you won't get flogged so much. Now, when you have visitors—two weeks after you go to Hiro—make sure that your mother doesn't bring you anything to eat. Tell all the other men in your barrack that. Otherwise, you'll have to crawl around the barrack and be kicked in the face, and . . ." I stopped. Tatsuno wasn't looking well.

He forced a wry smile. "It sounds like fun."

"It's not so bad, Tatsuno-*kun!*" I put an arm around his shoulder. "We'll probably get more punishment than you will, in flying school, and—"

"Yasuo," he interrupted, "remember how we used to dream of flying together—fighter pilots—in the same squadron?" I nodded. "It's hard to imagine that now. You're so far ahead of me. I doubt that we'll ever be together. I know that you'll be a fighter pilot, but me—I don't know. I feel funny. Right now—" He shook his head, and his voice was hoarse—"Right now, I'm scared. You're, you're the only person I'd ever tell that to, Yasuo."

I looked him in the eye. "Listen, don't you think I felt the same way, just three months ago? No, I didn't go around telling everybody how scared I was. But I was scared, very scared! It's the same with every man that goes in. I don't care who he is; just between you and me, he's scared. Three months of basic seems a long time when you are looking ahead, but it's not long when you're sitting here looking back."

"I envy you, right now," Tatsuno said, and stared at a scab on my chin.

"Yes," I admitted, "but look at it this way. Three months of basic, then six months of flying school . . . yes, they seem like a long time. Once we're out, though, once we're flying, a few months won't make any difference. Just think, within a year both of us will be fighter pilots—maybe flying together."

"I hope so."

"Come on," I prodded him, "we've always been a team, haven't we?"

He nodded, sat pensive, then said, "I guess I'd better be going."

"Meet you in the morning," I called. "I'll be going over to school for a while."

The sudden attention of family, relatives and friends was gratifying. Rapidly I felt myself becoming a hero. During my first day at home I had said all the patriotic platitudes that were expected. I had felt determined, courageous, and I now viewed the hell of basic in a different light. Late that night, having talked lengthily with father and Toshifumi, I went to sleep, elated and proud.

The following morning I walked to school with Tatsuno, and was greeted as though I had already performed mighty deeds. Daily, before classes commenced, a general assembly was held in the auditorium. During my visit, preliminary announcements were dispensed with, and I was asked to address the students. The thought of speaking extemporaneously frightened me, but several insistent teachers ushered me forward amid much cheering from the audience.

To my own surprise, I spoke easily for about fifteen minutes. Aside from some casual comments about the training, I never mentioned The Pig, *Taiko Binta*, the deserters, or the suicides. One simply didn't mention such things in public. Instead I described the rigors of combat training and talked of the classwork. I spoke of our divine heritage as sons of Nippon, of our future, and the obligation of all able-bodied young men. Closing, I bowed to a thunderous applause.

Following this, my weathered old principal, Hori-*san*, spoke briefly, saying, "This school is honored and proud to have helped mold such an outstanding young man. With interest we will follow his future accomplishments, and rejoice as he continues to discharge his sacred obligation to our emperor, to our country. May many of you students sitting here today follow in his path."

I left Onomichi High, not knowing that I would next see it under very different circumstances.

The remainder of that day I visited a few friends, one of whom was entering the marines, then spent the final hours with my family. We spoke at length of Shigeru, my second brother. No word from him for weeks, and our concern was increasing. As a captain in the counter-intelligence in Java, he could reveal nothing regarding his work. Some time before, in one of his rare messages, he had merely mentioned being well. "If you should not hear from me again," he had concluded, "I will await your visit to the *Yasukuni Jinja*"—the national shrine for military dead.

Shortly after supper we saw Toshifumi off, on his train for Tokyo. The time had vanished with incredible speed. I had barely found time to breathe, and now my leave was over. Just before midnight I told mother and Tomika *sayonara*— for the third time in three months. And even though I was

70

returning with greater confidence, I concluded then that farewells never get much easier.

Father accompanied me to the station where, to my surprise, a crowd of some two hundred and fifty students were awaiting me—a brass band playing. Shouts arose at our approach and a cordon of friends pressed in to offer their goodbys. Father had never looked prouder.

I was presented with gifts, including the school pennant and several autographed flags of Japan. Many of those students had actually cut their own fingers and signed their names with blood—a token of eternal friendship. I was to wear those mementos as scarves into battle.

From time to time I glanced at the train. "Well," I said, "maybe I'd better . . ."

"Yasuo!" someone called. It was Tatsuno, on the crowd's fringe, wriggling toward me. In a moment we were clasping each other like brothers. "I'll be seeing you soon, Tatsuno-*kun*," I said. "Remember what I told you!"

"Speech, Kuwahara, speech!" someone yelled, and the rest chimed in.

I tried to dissuade them, all to no avail. The band was playing *Light of the Firefly*—a bit blatantly, a bit off key. but it brought back a tide of memories, and my eyes began to smart. Watching their smiling faces I mumbled, "I hope many of you will follow me."

Then the conductor's voice, a complaining twang, was sounding the departure.

Moments later as the train clicked toward Hiro I was still hearing father's parting admonition: "In all things conduct yourself with honor, my son. Remember now that your life is no longer your own. If you should ever fall into dishonor . . . do not return to bring unhappiness and shame upon us. Live proudly, fight gloriously for the emperor. Should you die . . . I will have a grave prepared." Gripping my hand fiercely, he had asked, "Do you know my heart?"

As the train tunneled into the night I watched my own reflection in the window—a transparent ghost of me, through which I could see the receding lights of town. Suddenly I felt a need to remember everything, to lodge somewhere in my mind a picture of past things—family, friends, and places, the ocean on a wintry day, mountains, and rice fields.

71

Part Three

11

THE PRAYING MANTIS

Flying school, as I had anticipated, was better than basic. Even though the punishment continued, we had formed friendships and were hardened, both physically and mentally.

I was overjoyed to find that all the men in our original group were assigned to another four-section barracks together. Each section housed fifteen men as before, only this time our quarters were a little better, and we lived on a separate section of the base, next to the pilots. The pilots, most of them not much older than the rest of us, were an audacious, proud lot in our eyes. Daily we watched their flight performances with admiration. They were the eagles who would play an important role in bringing victory.

We were now designated as the Fourth Squadron and the first portion of our six-month course involved an intensified study of aeronautics. We also began learning to parachute. It wasn't until three months had elapsed that we began to fly the Akatombo (Red Dragonfly), a small biplane with two cockpits, for instructor and student.

Our new *hancho* treated us no better than The Pig and his comrades had. Rentaro Namoto, our first sergeant and flight instructor, we dubbed "Praying Mantis" because of his gangly, insect-like appearance and vicious nature. There were fewer dimensions to The Mantis' personality. He rarely joked, and I don't recall his laughing much. But there was no denying his cunning or his courage. Tall for a Japanese, with a supple, whip-like body, hatchet face, and reptilian eyes, Namoto was the coldest, most calculating man I have ever known. When he inflicted punishment it was always without emotion. He was a machine, methodical and precise.

During most of basic training we had been utterly bewildered and terrified. The sudden insecurity because of being uprooted from our familes, the fear of the unknown, the softness of our minds and bodies, the humiliation of being

72

just so many nameless digits—all had combined to make life a nightmare.

By flying school, however, we were undergoing a metamorphosis. In surreptitious ways we began striking back at the tyrants over us. Of course, few crimes are greater in the military, particularly the Japanese military, than disobedience. To disobey an authority, to retaliate, brought swift and dire punishment. However, subtle disobedience and retaliation were never viewed in quite the same light as the overt.

Raw defiance of authority meant violent retribution, perhaps complete destruction. It was not only flagrant disobedience, but a direct attempt to humiliate one's superior. To defy a *hancho* openly had terrible implications. It meant that one was also defying the commanding officer, the *Daihonei* in Tokyo, even the emperor himself.

Our subtlest misdeeds, on the other hand, were more in keeping with the general Japanese make-up woven with the covert and cunning. Although never acknowledged as such, our chicanery with The Mantis developed into something of a game and was usually repaid at a high rate of interest.

Our first trick was played one day before evening mess, just after we had received a battering with rifle butts. At each meal KP's were required to carry food to the *hancho* in their individual quarters. Several of the more intrepid men from our squadron, including Nakamura, Oka, Yamamoto and myself, had concocted a plan. One evening we accosted the KP on his way to The Mantis' quarters, and Oka hissed, *"Yai!* Wait up! We have some seasoning for the *hancho* rice."

"Huh?" the KP said. "Hey, you'd better not do anything. Look now, don't do that. Don't! Don't! Do you want to get me killed?"

"He'll never know a thing," Nakamura whispered, "if you'll just stop squealing like a pregnant mouse for a minute." In turn, all of us were vigorously massaging and scratching our heads over the steaming bowl of rice. Despite the KP's terrified protests we managed to deposit a goodly quantity of dandruff in the bowl. "Now," Nakamura patted his forlorn shoulder, "mix the seasoning in well. This is our special gift to the Mantis." The KP did as instructed, shaking his head and uttering a few appropriate curses.

Secluding ourselves, we watched him enter The Mantis'

73

room. There was no sound, and a second later he returned empty-handed. "Is he eating his rice?" I asked.

"Yes, yes, yes," the KP growled and stalked back toward the mess hall.

"Hey, does he like it?" Oka called from the barrack doorway. "Did he kiss your hand?" No answer.

This was truly a wonderful way of retaliating. It didn't matter to us that The Mantis was unaware of his humiliation. The important fact existed that he *was* being humiliated. That he was unaware of the indignity made it all the better. This way there would be no reprisal.

So successful had been our first rice-seasoning escapade that we determined to follow the same procedure regularly. Almost every evening we seasoned The Mantis' supper in like manner. After a time, Oka ingeniously suggested that we use a little human excrement for variety. We were seriously pondering the idea when something happened.

Moriyama, one of the KP's, was especially leery one evening when nearly a dozen of us approached him. "All of you can't put dandruff in the rice," he moaned. "The Mantis will see it. Why don't we forget about it for a while? You're overdoing it. You really are."

As usual Oka and Yamamoto were irrepressible. "Oh yes," Yamamoto said, "why don't we forget about it for a while— just because you happen to be on KP. We'll all be taking our turn at KP. We'll all have to do it. Don't be a boob."

"Well," Moriyama wavered, "don't all of you put your dandruff in. You'll flood the bowl over."

"No, no, we need every man," Nakamura declared. "Some of us are running out of dandruff!" Without further ado he began briskly rubbing his head over the rice. "Next, please," he said, and I stepped forward. Despite Moriyama's pleading, each man followed suit.

"Now mix it in, Moriyama," I told him, "if you don't want The Mantis to know."

"Mix it with what," he whined. "I've got to hurry or he'll be coming out."

"Use your hands, naturally," I advised.

"Great God, but this is hot!" Moriyama probed at the food with his fingers, wincing.

"Brave *samurai*," Oka soothed. "Be a brave, brave *samurai*."

The unhappy KP continued his task grimacing. "Now, what do I wipe my hands on?"

"Lick them off," someone suggested.

Moriyama opened his mouth to lick them, then stopped as if frozen, tongue half-extended. All twelve of us shook, some of us holding our own mouths to suppress the laughter. "*Bakayaro!*" Moriyama cursed, and then entered The Mantis' room, like a man approaching the guillotine.

With the door slightly ajar, we pressed close by the wall, listening intently. Moriyama and The Mantis exchanged a few words I couldn't make out. Then, Moriyama had apparently turned to go when The Mantis said, "Kindly wait a minute, my dear friend."

"Yes, sir!" Moriyama's voice quavered.

There was a long silence. Finally we could hear The Mantis saying, "This rice—it stinks. What makes it so oily? It stinks like hell! Where did you get it, from the latrine?"

"Let's get out of here," Nakamura suggested wisely and we shuffled quickly down the hall and around the corner near the outer door. A moment later we heard a crash and, in another instant, what sounded like a terrific boot in the rear. "Quick, outside!" I hissed. At that moment Moriyama stumbled toward us, with the remains of The Mantis' dinner plastered to the back of his head, dribbling down his neck and face.

"We're in for it now," he gasped, "all of us! He'll kill all of us!"

No one had anything to say this time. We merely watched as he moved off toward the latrine.

Having been found out, we awaited The Mantis' reaction with fear and trembling. It came the next day and was not so terrible as we had expected. At reveille formation The Mantis surveyed us all quietly. Not a man stirred. "It appears—" he said. Just then a formation of fighters surged directly over us and circled to land. "Eyes straight ahead!" he bellowed, then casually watched as the first plane settled on the strip, and lurched, screeching rubber. "Doesn't know how to land too well, does he?" This he said more to himself than anyone else. "As I was saying," he continued, "it appears that some of you men are concerned about my health. You've been supplementing my diet. Maybe you think I'm too thin! In any case—those of you who have been so concerned—I want you to know that I appreciate your

75

every kindness. I suppose it is only natural to love your instructors. When I was a trainee, we loved our instructors. We were concerned about their health just as you are."

Oka made a slight strangling noise. "Shh!" I warned.

The Mantis continued, "However, you can rest at ease. We instructors are well fed, and you have no need for concern. As a matter of fact, last night, when our KP brought my dinner, I wasn't even hungry. I gave it all back to him. He was a terribly sloppy eater, though.

Both Oka and Yamamoto wheezed this time. "Now this morning," he went on, "just to show you I am appreciative, I propose a toast. *Hancho* Kitimura! *Hancho* Maki!" Two *hancho* hastened among us, distributing small *sake* cups. "Be at ease!" The Mantis said. Astonished, we watched as they began to fill cups from a gigantic blue bottle. "*Dozo*, fine," The Mantis said when they had finished. "Wonderful, Awamori *sake* all the way from Okinawa!" I was dumbfounded, Could this really be? Soberly he said, "And now, I propose a toast to all of you. To the men of the Fourth Squadron."

"*Kampai!* Bottoms up! To the men of the Fourth Squadron!" we rumbled in unison.

It took a while to register. Each man's lips had suddenly turned blue. The awful-tasting stuff was ink!

For a while we played no more tricks. Tatsuno had arrived at Hiro and was undergoing the hell of early basic, living in the same quarters I had. He had known what to expect, though, and had prepared himself as well as possible. Our visits were rare because neither of us had much free time. Also, men were not allowed to enter any barrack other than their own. I was quietly talking with Tatsuno one night outside his quarters when The Pig passed us carrying several ball bats. I didn't think he'd notice me but, leaning the bats against the wall, he remarked, "*Ah so!* Kuwahara has returned. You see how attached these men become to their first home away from home. They love it; they can't stay away—*na*, Kuwahara?" He gave my shoulder a kindly pat as he entered the barrack.

"*Ha*, honorable *hancho-dono*," I grinned. I no longer hated The Pig, and I felt a minor thrill at being regarded a little more as his equal.

"Looks as if we're going to get some more fighting spirit from The Pig," Tatsuno said. "I'd better go on in."

"Stay outside a minute," I said. "If he herds them out now,

there won't even be a roll call. It's not even eight o'clock. He won't notice whether you're missing." Tatsuno was understandably fearful, but I suggested that he come back with me behind some shrubbery about thirty yards beyond the barrack. "If they start calling the roll," I said, "you can just walk up and get into formation."

Still doubtful, he relaxed. We strolled back and sat down behind the bushes. To our surprise nothing happened. After a while The Pig emerged and disappeared in the direction of his own quarters. "There goes the strangest man I have ever known," I said.

We remained there, conversing until nearly time for *Shoto Rappa*, then parted.

The first three months of flight school went far more rapidly than basic training, and I was truly learning to fly. At long last I was actually in a power-driven plane. I'll never forget those first days in the Akatombo. I took to the new trainers as readily as I had taken to the gliders. I had studied aeronautics zealously, and time after time The Mantis or one of the other instructors warned me against being too eager. So thoroughly had I familiarized myself with the instrument board, the entire flight operation, I had secretly felt that I could take off and land, unassisted, on my very first attempt.

During my hours in the air, watching the earth change and roll beneath me, I felt an exhilaration, a power that dispelled all the unpleasant and painful experiences. Unhappiness was something that belonged to the ground. The skies were a totally different realm. Nothing could hurt me in the sky. I belonged there.

Our hours on the ground were a vivid contrast. Steadily, relentlessly, The Mantis poured on the punishment. Because it took more to break us, he gave us more, and a general bitterness was growing. More than one man threatened to kill him. How it was accomplished I don't know, but someone even managed to procure some poison. Several men were determined to use it on our taskmaster, and not without some heated arguments were they dissuaded.

We did, however, begin striking back with greater vigor and less subtlety than before. Four or five of us were usually at the root of these retaliations, and no sooner were we punished for one scheme than we began to weave others.

The Mantis had a huge whip, which he cracked at the

slightest provocation. He handled it with real finesse, and with little exertion was able to inflict excruciating pain.

One day after we had all received a terrible lashing we met in the latrine to concoct a plan. Late each night The Mantis would return from town, where he had been drinking and carousing with the prostitutes. It was said that liquor and women were the very air he breathed. He would sop up prodigious quantities of alcohol nightly and show no effect the next morning. His capacity for women was supposedly even greater. According to one of the fighter pilots, The Mantis was a satyr supreme, who performed impossible sexual feats, whose fire was never quenched. All this seemed to contradict our concept of that fish-cold, metal-eyed personality with whom we had to cope during the daylight hours.

Nevertheless we decided to take advantage of his absences. Almost nightly at about twelve o'clock our instructor would weave along the hall crunching down the short flight of steps to his room at the far end of the barrack.

The night of our new plan found a handful of us awake and waiting, listening attentively inside our own quarters. For a long time nothing happened and the minutes writhed by. The hour was midnight, and still no Mantis. "Maybe he didn't leave the base tonight," I suggested.

"Yes he did," Nakamura assured me. "I saw him leave right after mess."

"Yes," Oka said boisterously, "The Mantis would never miss his—you know what!"

Sleep kept asserting itself, and it was settling on us like a fog when the barrack door opened. Footsteps echoed along the dimly lit hall, and a moment later there was a resounding crash. We crawled into our cots frightened, but very, very pleased. The taut wire across the stairway had done its job.

The next morning The Mantis had a bandage across his nose. Never cracking the faintest smile, as usual, he said, "I am happy to note that some of you men are practical jokers. A good sense of humor is often very refreshing." All of the Fourth Squadron knew by then what had happened. "Today," he continued, "I have prepared a little joke also—just to show you I'm not thoughtless and unappreciative. This afternoon for physical training, when it is pleasant and warm, you will wear your nice flying suits. Humorous, *ha?*"

We awaited the afternoon with trepidation. During the morning our instructor scarcely laid a hand on us—definitely the lull before a storm. The fated time arrived and, true to his word, The Mantis had us don all our flying accoutrements: our feather-lined suits, boots, leather helmets, scarves, and parachute packs. Heat waves were shimmering out on the airstrip as we commenced our usual hour of calisthenics. For the first few minutes our flying suits served as protection from the sun. One or two of the men even maintained that we should always wear flying suits. I was dubious, for the first drops of sweat had formed under my arms. The heat was building from within, with no means of escape. "In about five minutes you'll know how crazy you are," I informed one of the more optimistic.

"Come now, Kuwahara," he said, "don't always be such a pessimist."

As we did push-ups, side by side, I grunted, "In a minute you'll be changing your mind, my friend."

"No, I won't!"

"Fool!"

"Boob!"

Never since I had entered Hiro had anyone intimated that I was a boob. Unreasonably furious, I got to my feet. "Stand up, *shinpei*," I said, "and we'll see who the boob is."

Obligingly, he got to his feet, grinning impudently. I struck with all my strength staggering him, at the same time losing my balance. We fell in a tangle among the other men, grappling awkwardly. There were curses. We were grabbed and separated. Yamamoto had hold of my arms. "Do you want to get us all killed?" he said.

Then The Mantis was among us with his lash, but with little effect, we were so well padded. As we stood awaiting the next exercises, I realized how stupid I had been. Already burning up inside, I was panting, my throat dust-dry. Sweat was seeping from my forehead into my eyes, blurring the backs before me. My whole body was quivering, and my legs felt hollow. I couldn't bring myself to look at Tanaka, the man I had fought.

By the time our calisthenics terminated we were boiling in our suits. But then the daily run around the strip began. It was difficult enough even moving fast in the heavy clothing, but the heat was tremendous. The body heat was continuing to build from within and the sun blazed against the outer leather. Just before our run I had slipped off a glove. The leather actually burned my hand. And now we were lumbering down the long cement stretch, The Mantis pedaling comfortably along on his bicycle. The land of concrete and sun seemed to stretch on and on, and I remembered a statement from our commanding officer: "The Imperial Way is a long way, never-ending. It will never end."

"Long, long, long . . ." the words began repeating. Through the sweat I could see only a short distance. "Long, long, long . . ." The Japanese way of life . . . it would fill all the world. That was why it had to be such a long, hard way. Minute after minute the boots clumped rhythmically. How had I ever come by the notion that there was any end to this airfield? I didn't remember turning. Which direction were we going? That's right, it was never-ending. "Long, long, long . . ." Somehow I felt that there were fewer men behind us now. Ahead someone pitched and hit the cement rolling. The runway was rocking now. Thirty seconds later another man held his stomach, staggered and went down. He rolled off to the side and, as I passed by, it struck me that he was sinking like a ship in the sea. Only he was sinking into the concrete. Another man going down now, tripping the man behind him. Yes, they were both sinking into the concrete. That was good. Their bodies would become part of the concrete. Years from now men would break up this strip to make a new one, and they would find hollow statues. But even then I would still be running beneath the sun far ahead. Oka, Yamamoto, even Nakamura—they would be statues. It was sad. But, to be a statue! If I were a statue with the rest I could be taken home to the family shrine. I could sit in the cool of the evening under the trees among the flowers, the cicadas humming, and Tomika would come quietly to pour water on me. She would whisper, "My little brother."

I never felt the concrete rising to meet me. Tepid liquid from a canteen splashed against my face. I saw the spokes of a bicycle wheel turning by.

12

A FULL REPARATION

For some days we devised no more schemes. Too well we had felt the impact of The Mantis' jokes. Again, someone had obtained poison. Again, arguments had arisen. "I don't care what they do to me," the would-be assassin had muttered. "At least that inhuman *chikusyo* (beast) will get what's coming to him!"

"Yes, but the whole squadron will get it worse," another had reminded him. The poison was poured down the toilet after a day or two.

Barely a week after the flying-suit episode I had my first unpleasant air experience. Our rancor against The Mantis had reached the crest of another wave, and we were contemplating more games. How could we humiliate him and still remain undetected? That was the vital question. Something a bit more subtle than tripping him down the stairs this time. "How about a good, strong laxative in his food?" Nakamura suggested.

"Ha! You think we wouldn't get caught?" I asked.

"Sleeping pills!" Tanaka cried triumphantly. "How about sleeping pills? He'd never make it up for formation. He'd be broken!"

"That would be good," someone else agreed. "The Mantis a *shinpei!* Wouldn't he get it?"

"He'd probably go over the fence the first day!"

"No . . ." I shook my head. "I don't care what else you say about him, he is tough. The Mantis would never break."

"Aaa," Tanaka said, "he'd bawl for his mother the first day. He'd go hang himself." I looked at Tanaka and fought down an old anger. The feeling had been there ever since our scrap on the airstrip. One thing I could count on with Tanaka—we would never agree, not on anything. And always, that impudent grin. I could see myself smashing his face in, changing it so his mother wouldn't even know him —except for one thing. The grin would still be there.

"All right, *shinpei,*" I said, "you go ahead and get the sleeping pills. We'll see how it works out."

"All right, *shinpei,*" he replied and made an exaggerated bow.

Despite our animosity, I found myself eagerly awaiting the results of Tanaka's project. Unfortunately he was never able to procure the necessary pills. How anybody had managed to obtain poison was a mystery which most of us never unraveled.

Before long a new plan had unfolded, however. Tatsuno was weathering his basic admirably, and I was truly proud of him. He was small and pale and it was true he always ap-

81

peared on the verge of some serious malady, but somehow Tatsuno always stuck to a thing. Even when it seemed that the faintest breeze might sweep him away, he kept clinging, even when bigger men gave up.

On a dark night Nakamura and I met with Tatsuno and one of his new friends in a latrine. "Now this is our plan," I whispered. "We'll help you fix your *hancho,* if you'll help us fix ours. What we need right now are some needles. We want the needles from every sewing kit in your barrack. Nobody will ever inspect the inside of your sewing kits, anyway. You'll get them back when we're through with them— I hope!" I then revealed our scheme. A day later we had the needles.

Shortly after ten one night we skulked into our leader's room, turned back the covers on his bed, and began planting the needles head-downward in his mattress, the points projecting approximately an inch above the surface. We then re-made the bed, stretching the under sheet and blanket so taut that the points were not exposed.

Hastening to our quarters, we sat in the dark and chuckled. "I trust he will have a good night's rest," I hissed.

"They sleep that way in India," Yamamoto said. "We can't have them outdoing us." That night we were brimming with laughter. "Hey, hey, look at me," Oka said. "I'm The Mantis!" A marvelous performance. He staggered down the dark aisle, clumsily removed his clothing, then yawned blissfully and stretched. "Good night, my children. Pleasant dreams," he murmured, slowly lying back. We watched closely in the dim light as Oka's eyes closed. Suddenly they popped open, bulging, and his mouth formed a silent, agonized scream. For several seconds his legs and arms flailed, then he catapulted from his cot and began to spring up and down as though he were on a diving board.

It was always fun to watch either Yamamoto or Oka act up, for both of them were as quick and wiry as squirrels. Oka's ludicrous routine convulsed us until we cried. Others began their own performances and soon all fifteen men in our section were awake, listening. "What this time?" someone groaned.

I heard Moriyama reply, "Oh, Oka and Kuwahara and the rest of their *gokudo* . . . they're just getting the whole squadron into trouble again." It was after eleven when we quieted down.

After morning mess, all the men from our quarters were summoned to The Mantis' room. Idly drumming his fingers on a chair arm, he tilted back and eyed us silently. Sticking from the top of his table in four neat, silver rows were sixty needles.

For a long time he sat as if meditating. At length he plucked a needle from the table, and sighted at a spot on the wall with it, closing one eye. "Well?" he said. No one responded. "We never thought of this one when I was in school. Very clever. Yes, very clever!" Suddenly his chair slammed into an upright position. Eying us soberly, shaking his head, he said, "And you don't know a thing about this, do you?" Stiffening, he pointed at Nakamura. "You, pimple-face! Let's have an answer!"

Nakamura swallowed, but couldn't speak.

"Splendid! A nice, direct answer. It is strange, though, my fine pimple-face, that you manifest no surprise, no lack of understanding. Apparently you know what I'm referring to —correct?"

"No, honorable *hancho-dono!*"

The Mantis arose and began pacing about. Once he paused before Moriyama, staring at him through icy eyes. "No, no . . . you wouldn't know, would you? Too stupid!" Casually he flipped Moriyama's nose. Then we were dismissed.

As we filed out he called, "Just one minor detail: every single man in this squadron will bring his sewing kit to the next formation. See that the other barracks are informed."

Upon later discovering that every one of our kits contained a needle, The Mantis appeared impassive. He merely complimented us upon our strategy and added that he had prepared a special token of his appreciation.

Again, the first part of the day passed tranquilly; even the physical training passed without a hitch.

Then it came time for our daily flying lesson. "Two weeks ago, I believe that some of you became rather warm in your flying suits," the Mantis announced, "even a trifle weary, shall we say. Today, just to show you what a grand fellow I am, we will forego the hot suits. How does that sound?"

As I climbed into the rear cockpit, the instructor before me turned, and I hadn't noticed who he was until then. It was my old friend from basic, The Snake. He'd been transferred. I began to fasten my safety belt, but he shook his head. "No safety belts allowed, Kuwahara—sorry!" I was taken aback—no safety belt! Also The Snake had spoken as though he liked me. That was equally startling.

We took off, climbing rapidly. At about five thousand feet, he glanced back grinning, his eyes mere slits through the goggles. "Hang on!" Already the chill air was buffeting me through the open cockpit.

Seizing the dead controls, I watched the world turn upside down—felt it rushing toward us. We were turning a lazy loop. I pulled my head against my chest and grasped the loose safety straps. Black spots jumped at me. We were leveling out, slicing into a cloud bank. The wind ripped in, numbing me. Then, emerging from the vapor, we began a second loop. No belt! Like a tremendous hand, the air wrenched and tore at me. A moment more and I'd be flung into the sky! Grimly I battled with gravity, and the tearing, freezing wind.

When at length we leveled out, I wasn't sure which side was up. Before I could regain my breath we had nosed over into a downward spiral. As though I had suddenly drunk too much ice water, my forehead began to throb. Vision blurred and darkness closed in. When I came to, we were preparing to land. Unable to move, I was hauled from the plane.

All sixty of us took special rides that day, and for nearly half an hour after, most of us were unable to stand. We were so done in, as a matter of fact, that The Mantis half-apologized. "After all, men this *is* the air force. You must accustom yourselves to things like this."

But this was not to be my last unpleasant flight in an Akatombo, not by any means. For only a short time later, about two weeks after my solo flight, an amazing, inexplicable thing happened. Six of us were flying in formation, when The Mantis commanded us to play "follow the leader" with him. First in line, I followed close behind as he slipped into a bank, a gentle dive, and began to loop. I followed him all the way, and pulled out of my own loop close on his tail. For some reason, a reason that still mystifies me, instead of slowing I speeded up.

Sensing our proximity, The Mantis veered and began climbing. I followed precariously near. It was an odd sensation. I seemed to have no control over myself. All at once words were screaming in my phones, "Get off my tail, you madman! You stupid fool! Drop back!"

Already the rest of the flight was trailing at a distance. The Mantis slid into a steep dive, and I went after him as though attached by a cable. Had he been flying a faster, more maneuverable craft I never would have stayed with him. But his attempts to escape in the trainer were futile—twisting, rolling, climbing and diving. It was impossible to shake me. The idea of crashing him, snuffing him out in the air suddenly had an overwhelming appeal. Simultaneously I was terrified, as if compelled to follow a mesmerist.

As we cut a tight, left circle The Mantis bawled, "Turn right! Turn right!" The order, to me, was no more than the buzz of a trapped fly. I turned left, and we missed colliding by a sliver.

Desperately, The Mantis headed full throttle for the mountains above Fukagawa, and soon we were roaring between their shoulders, low along the valleys. A bearded incline towered before us. I pulled back on the stick, saw The Mantis climb—almost too late! His wing nicked off the tip of a pine! Still I followed, the victim of a relentless compulsion as we continued the climb—barely apart. Now above the first peak, we were circling.

Then it happened! Uttering a final, frantic oath, The Mantis bailed out. I watched the silken mushroom billow, snapping a doll-sized figure. Smaller and smaller it grew. The Mantis was being wafted gently across a valley when something flashed a long way off. The Akatombo had come to rest.

By now my head was roaring, my body turned to honeycomb. Probably I would have crashed somewhere, had not a voice come over the phones: "Kuwahara! Come back! Turn back! Don't do anything you'll regret. Remember your family! Remember the emperor! You have an obligation!" It was The Snake circling above.

The entire episode, like dream fragments, had only lasted a few minutes. Somehow I joined the main formation. Sanity returned, and with it an awful fear. Trembling, I went through the remaining exercises, the terror growing. Shortly after landing, I was taken before the commanding officer. Our frolic over the mountains of Fukagawa had quickly attracted a good deal of attention.

The Mantis was already there, unhurt, having been picked up by the ambulance. It was a weird situation. As soon as I had reported to the commanding officer, he bade us sit down, the proceedings were conducted with surprising informality. Obviously fascinated with my actions, seemingly more for his own information than anything else, he said, "Now, let us determine precisely what happened. We will hear from you first, Namoto."

The Mantis glared at me sidelong. "Honorable commanding officer, I must tell you that this man is insane! Obviously! During a routine flight practice he did everything in his power to ram me. Had I not bailed out, he would have succeeded. He—"

"Just how long did he chase you?"

"For several minutes, honorable commanding officer. He—"

"An inexperienced trainee, and you were unable to elude him?"

"I—"

"Curious. . . . A good many strange things have occurred since I came to Hiro, but never, never anything quite like this." He picked up a pencil, poised it over a paper pad, then twirled it between his fingers and began drumming it on the desk top. For a moment he smiled. "Of course, we've lost a *hancho* or two from time to time." The Mantis stiffened slightly. Still drumming his pencil, without looking up, the commanding officer asked, "What do you have to say about this, private Kuwahara?"

I stammered and stared at my feet. "I, I have nothing to say, honorable commanding officer." What could I say? How could anyone explain such a thing?

"Was it your intention to kill this man?"

"No . . ."

"Were you trying to show off, for the other men?"

"No, I—"

"Honorable commanding officer!" The Mantis snapped at me, but our inquisitor silenced him with a quick, almost irritated, gesture.

"Hmmm, when did you decide to do this thing?"

I swallowed. "I didn't. I mean, I don't know, honorable commanding officer. I just followed—as he instructed us to. I—I just followed him."

"I see. Weren't you following a bit too close for comfort? Apparently Sergeant Namoto thought so. He was so uncomfortable that he bailed out, and permitted one of our perfectly good trainers to crash." Muscles in The Mantis' jaw tightened.

"I am sorry, honorable commanding officer," I said, and realized how foolish I sounded. But there was nothing else to say. The Mantis had commanded us to play follow the leader. I had followed.

For some time the officer sat mute. Once he massaged his brow. Once he shook his head and swore softly. The commander was a small man, one who would pass unnoticed even on the streets of Onomichi. But the military environment seemed to bring out the bigness in him. His whole bearing, the gestures, the quiet strength indicated a big man in a small man's body.

"Do you know what I wanted to be, back when I started college?" he asked. "I wanted to be . . . as a matter of fact, I was determined to be . . . a psychiatrist. But . . ." He lit a cigarette and squinted, expelling the smoke. "You know how it goes. Costs a lot of *okane.*"

After a while he said, "Perhaps, private, you are like I was. My mother worked like a slave to buy me a bicycle." He seemed to be looking back. "I was—oh, not more than ten— my father dead. Anyway, my brother was going to teach me how to ride it. (He already had a bicycle—stole it, as I recall.) Anyway, he was going to teach me how to ride it. 'Follow me,' he told me. 'Just do everything I do!' " The commander chuckled a little. "This was practically before I even knew how to balance the crazy thing, see. Well, we were going along the road, out in the country, and I was doing all right. Every time I asked a question: 'Just follow me. Do everything I do.' That's all he would say—crazy, damned brother! Well, I got to following him too closely, see, and I must have hit a rock, because all at once I turned into his rear wheel, and down we went—right into a newly dunged rice paddy!"

Suddenly, all three of us fell to laughing—three comrades. It was the first time I had ever heard the Mantis laugh.

"Ha! 'Just do everything I do!' For the next few days we were about ostracized, and I had to find a new teacher."

We laughed again. Then the conversation ended.

We were dismissed and I was sent to the guardhouse to "think things over." Certainly the commanding officer had treated me with astonishing consideration, but The Mantis did his best to balance the scales. Quietly he ushered me into the guardhouse. "Maybe that stupid commander doesn't intend that you should make a reparation, Kuwahara . . ." Then I saw it, a club. "But believe me, you shall. For this indignity, you shall be repaid in full! I raised my arm toward off the blow, but it came too fast, too hard.

There was an explosion in my brain, and I seemed to hear the sound of wood against my skull—hear it with my whole body. Then a black hole swallowed me. No pain at all.

Whether I lay for minutes or hours it is impossible to tell. Gradually I began to be aware of sensations, but for a time I was no particular person—just a glimmer of something in an area of unfeeling. Cold, cold. Eventually words formed: "What am I doing in the ocean?" It occurred to me that I was dead. When you are dead they bury you beneath the earth, but somehow you just keep sinking, sinking until you come out in the ocean. You just lie quietly at the bottom of the ocean. It doesn't hurt, not if you lie quietly. It's just dark and cold, very cold. It's terribly hard, though. Why must it be so hard?

I was lying face down, slowly pushing my hands out over the cement floor. A floor! Then I began to remember. For a moment I couldn't recall how or why, but I had humiliated someone. Finally the words returned: "For this indignity you shall be repaid in full." Gradually my brain began to clear. Still I just lay there—no sense moving. The floor was not only cold, but damp, and I kept tasting something like sea water. I felt my face. It was beginning to throb. Above my left ear was a swelling, more of a welt than a lump. Again I touched my face. It was covered with dried blood. After I had fallen The Mantis had apparently used his feet.

Sitting up, I stared at the oblong square of light on the floor. The light was sectioned. I glanced up to the barred window, struggled to my feet, and peered out. Evening now.

Hiro was quiet, except for the sound of a *hancho* marching recruits in the distance. The guardhouse was nothing but a square room—no table, no cot, no chair, not even a straw *tatami* to sit on. For several minutes I gripped the bars, looking out. When my legs began to sag I sat down and eased over into a corner, drawing my knees up, resting my head and arms on them. Anyway, I had humiliated The Mantis tremendously. In a way I had vindicated the entire Fourth Squadron. I had stuck with him in the air. No matter what he had done, I had stayed with him, broken that steel nerve. He had been convinced I was out to kill him.

A clicking at the door startled me. It opened slightly. A guard leaned inside and placed something on the floor. "Here's your chow, and a blanket," he said, and the door clanged shut. Not until then did I realize my hunger. I was ravenous.

Nothing but rice, pickles, and water, but I gulped it all down like an animal, smearing my whole chin. My face throbbed and it hurt to eat. But that didn't matter. Some rice fell on the floor and I carefully pinched it up, devouring it to the last kernel. Then I licked the bowl and my fingers.

The light pattern was dim on the floor now, lengthening. Spreading my thin blanket out on the floor. I lay on its outer edge, and rolled up in it. By rolling tight I could have two layers over and under me. A cold fall night was filtering through the bars, and I shivered. Hunching close to the wall, I fell asleep, thinking that the next day might see me free.

In this, however, I was woefully mistaken. My sojourn in the guardhouse turned out to be the worst experience of my entire training. All the next day I waited, hoping to be released. Only two incidents broke the emptiness of those hours. Once I was permitted to go to the latrine. In the evening the door opened again—another bowl of rice and pickles. This time I ate more slowly, carefully savoring each morsel. I tried to remember that food was unimportant. Really, it was one's attitude that counted. After all, hadn't the early *samurai* been able to go without food for days? When food was unavailable they would sit calmly, picking their teeth, pretending they had just finished a sumptous repast.

Finishing my own sumptuous repast, I rolled up once more in my blanket, intending, hoping, to sleep until the morning. Perhaps I could sleep most of the time away. After two hours of fitful dozing, though, I arose and began pacing about my cell. The floor had not grown any softer, nor had my special rolling-up technique kept the cold from penetrating.

My shoulder blades and hip bones were sore. One can only relax on concrete so long. The left side of my head was still wooden from the club blow and my eyes were black from The Mantis' feet. In a way I was glad that he had punished me so severely at first. Perhaps he would leave me alone now, until my release. Somehow I had acquired the notion that I would be there only for a day. But there in that second night I wondered. Maybe I would remain in the empty room for weeks.

"Kuwahara!"

I started. Had someone called me? Several times that day, words had sounded in my own mind. "Kuwahara! Hey, come over to the window!" No mistake this time. Undoubtedly my friends were concerned about me. Maybe they had brought some food.

Gripping the bars, I peered out. "Who is it?"

"Are you all right?" I heard. I became excited. "Let me see your face. Is it all right?"

Pressing my swollen visage partially through the bars, I whispered, "Nakamura? I'm here. Who is it?"

"It is I!" a fiendish voice snarled, and something cracked, searing my face like a torch. Screaming I staggered back, throwing my hands against the pain. The Mantis had crouched there with his whip. As I writhed on the floor he hissed, "Why carry on so, young bastard? I was merely checking to make sure that your face is all right."

The whip sting traveled from my mouth, up over my nose and across one eye. Tears were pouring from that eye profusely. It could see nothing. After several minutes I crawled over to my blanket and draped it about me. For hours I barely stroked and patted the hurt area. Each time I stopped it began to smart and burn fiercely. Between the hours of four and seven, I lost awareness of the pain from time to time. It must have been sleep, but it brought no satisfaction—just occasional blank spots.

Eventually light in the window turned from gray to blue. I got up and began walking back and forth. Far off on the strip, motors were revving—a wonderful sound. Suddenly a dismaying thought struck me. If I remained in the guardhouse much longer, my chances for making fighter school would be eliminated. The thought gave me a jolt, and just as my head began to swirl with fearful imaginings the door opened.

It was my friend, The Mantis. "Come over here!" he ordered. "Turn around!" So . . . another whipping. Well, I'd received plenty of those before. Grimly I told myself that it was at least a break in the monotony. But I was no more prepared for what happened then than I had been for the lash the night before.

The first blow slammed me to my hands and knees. The second flattened me on the floor. The Mantis was using a length of wet rope, about an inch and a half in diameter.

Time and again during that day the treatment was repeated. One lash usually knocked me down, and if it didn't render me unconscious, I fainted from pain anyway. Again and again and again . . . waiting from one lashing to the next, quivering and moaning, swearing, pleading to the God who had forgotten. When the guard opened the door for my daily trip to the latrine, I smothered a cry. When my usual supper came I cowered in the corner. For long minutes after the guard's departure I shook and gnawed on my knuckles. The rope treatment had been coming about every two hours.

Somehow the third day faded into the fourth. Early in the morning, rational thought returned. I began to wonder how The Mantis would react if the tables were turned. Could I make him cringe, grovel, plead for mercy? A delicious thought! But I doubted that it could be done. What would it take to make him plead?

For a moment I recalled our survival training in the mountains outside Hiro. The Mantis had kept us without sleep for nearly four days, without food for over two. I remembered the picture: grim recruits surrounding The Mantis with loaded pistols. And the man had shown no emotion whatsoever, not even the faintest trace of uneasiness. He had merely eyed them and remarked, "Why do that? You'll only get into trouble." When they had wavered, then backed down, he had added a casual afterthought: "After all, you have been learning how to eat and sleep ever since you were born. Now you must learn how *not* to eat and sleep."

And this was the man I had humiliated. He not only hated me but, as I dimly realized, he felt morally obligated to "repay me in full." True enough, he was a sadist, but my punishment would have been severe in any event. It is the moral duty of a Japanese to repay an injustice, as well as a favor.

Eventually my thoughts drifted once more to fighter school. It still mattered, more than ever now. For a while I could not remember how many days had passed. Maybe I could still make fighter school. Maybe. That was the only thing that mattered. I didn't even think of home.

Then the flash of optimism was gone. The door opened. By now I didn't care what happened. "Kill me!" I yelled hoarsely. "Kill me! Get it over with!"

Slowly he approached. "Get up, Kuwahara!"

"No!" I screamed. "No! No! No!"

"Get up!"

I cursed him: *"Konchikusyo! Bakayaro! Gaki!"*

He moved close, the rope readied. "All right, if you want it on the floor—" I thrashed out, kicking his shins. The Mantis then cursed me with every foul word he could think of, and he knew more than I did. But again, I had shattered his icy calm, and he hated me more than ever for it. I tried to roll away. The rope swished. Again the black oblivion opened, and I plunged in.

About two hours later the door opened again. I stared vacantly.

"Get up!"

"No," I barely croaked. The arm raised. Yes, there it was —the black hole again. The wonderful, blessed, great, dark hole!

By afternoon I lay thinking about the black hole. It was good, but it could hold me only so long. Always I would drift to the surface. Sometimes when the light began to increase, I'd swim down toward the depths, but each time it was a shorter stay. That hole and the dark corner of the cell had a relationship to each other. Why did I always have to return? Why couldn't I stay down? Why? Why? Then it came to me. I could stay down forever!

A sense of triumph filled me. Idly I began dragging about the room, crippled, but that didn't matter. I was looking for something. There was only one thing—my metal rice bowl. Possibly I could bend it some way, then grind it on the floor, grind it until it was sharp.

Holding the bowl sidewise, I began to flatten it with my heel. Plane motors were grumbling in the sky now, a continual crisscross of sound. I looked at the barred window and saw a dragonfly. Slowly I got to my feet and limped toward the light. The insect's wings made a strange, brittle sound as it danced into the day. The window ledge was shoulder-high, indented about six inches to the bars.

Then I knew that it would be a simple matter. A perfect ledge! Men had done it that way before—a bench, a table, a stair step, or a ledge—it made no difference. I locked my hands over my head. Yes, it would work perfectly. Simply stick my tongue out, clamp it between my teeth, lock my hands on my head. . . . Then! I would slam my chin on the ledge—hard, with all my strength. That way my tongue would be bitten off and I would bleed to death. Yes, more than one man had died that way at Hiro.

My hands still locked, I pushed my head down slowly, to see just where my chin would strike. This was no time for a mistake. Sticking my tongue out, I chewed tentatively. I was afraid, but not as afraid as I had thought I would be. It was interesting. I seemed to be slowly burning.

The dragonfly returned and balanced on the outer ledge. What was it I had learned in school? Something about how a caged dragonfly, without food, would eventually begin eating on its own tail, never stopping until it had devoured nearly half its body. Surely I could do a small thing like bite off my own tongue.

The immense, almond-shaped eyes. I had never realized that eyes could look like that. In fascination I stared at the shimmering, blue body—at the transparent filament wings. Why did it have four wings instead of two? I pushed my finger toward him. He flared away sidewise, balanced in the air, and was gone.

Blankly I stared into space. Then I looked down at my hands, and watched them open and close. My hands were shaped like my mother's. That was what she had always said. The nails had the same half-moons. Slowly I locked my hands over my head and felt the hair. It was dirty hair. It was sweaty. But it was mine. It was important. It was my own special hair. I held a palm against my forehead, stroked my fingers down over the nose and mouth. They were mine, and they were very special. The plane motors were louder than I had ever heard them.

I would wait for just a little while. Yes, I would kill myself, but I would wait just a little while. Slowly I sat down and began to cry.

13

FIGHTER PILOT

On the evening of the fourth day I was released, to be placed on latrine duty for a week. During that week I found that by simply groaning quietly to myself I could do a lot to soothe the pain. There wasn't much work involved, but I hobbled and limped about, mopping the floors, cleaning the toilets, more racked with soreness than I had ever been—even in the beginning stages of basic. The Mantis had beaten me either fifteen or sixteen times, I forget which.

My week of latrine duty was crucial. If I'd succumbed to the pain, I would have been hospitalized, thereby losing any chance for fighter school. Flight training was proceeding rapidly. At graduation we all would be assigned according to our aptitudes: fighter, bomber, signal, or mechanic school. Naturally, most of us aspired to the first. For me, not making fighter school would be a crushing blow. After all the pain, the struggle, the heartache—then to be consigned to mechanic or signal school. The idea was insufferable.

Had it not been for my friends I surely would have gone to the hospital. Each night Nakamura, Yamamoto and Oka would massage me with oil. Several times they even helped me clean the latrine—true acts of devotion. I was something of a hero in the Fourth Squadron now. Twice during the week Tatsuno visited me. He was faring well and would soon begin training in the Akatombo.

Somehow I weathered the week. Eleven days after the fateful air chase I was again in the skies. In the interim the others had progressed considerably, but I was still numbered among the better flyers. Curiously enough, The Mantis no longer indulged in follow-the-leader games. Undoubtedly the training had progressed too far by then for any such childish pursuits.

Each day I took to the sky more elated. I was a natural when it came to flying, and I knew it. It was the bird instinct that I had felt so strongly over Mt. Ikoma. There were no more attempts to humiliate The Mantis. The end was too near. Besides, the punishment abated slightly and moved along on an even keel. Even our *hancho* became weary from time to time.

As graduation neared I became increasingly excited. True, I was flying with the best in the squadron, making few mistakes. But still . . . The doubt and fear bored into me continually. No one knew exactly how many would be chosen for fighter school; there were only rumors. Some declared that only two or three top flyers would qualify. Others estimated that as many as twenty would make it. No matter what the time or the country, rumors always run rampant in the military.

Added to these doubts was the thought that I might not be selected because of my conduct against The Mantis. Still, though, the commanding officer hadn't seemed angry with me. He had only displayed a keen interest. And wasn't it true that very few men could follow a skilled instructor through the skies as I had? Optimism and pessimism were constantly clashing within me. With only a week left, the pressure became so great that I was in mental agony. If I failed . . . Well, it was obvious. Suicide would be the only possible way to atone.

Some of the others may not have felt as strongly about it as I, but the tension was mounting throughout the whole Fourth Squadron. Close friends flared at each other, sometimes fighting with the slightest provocation. Twice Oka and Yamamoto nearly came to blows, and it was all I could do to refrain from battling Tanaka each time he came near. Always the grin, and always the snide comments. It was something neither of us could explain, for we both had the same circle of associates.

Somehow we made it through the tension of those final days. Graduation was upon us and assignments were being issued. It was an autumn afternoon when I shouldered my way through a flock of eager companions. They were clustered about the orderly room bulletin board, peering, jabbering and exclaiming. Having read the orders, many of the men turned silently and walked away. Few of them registered any visible emotion, but from their very gait, from the incline of their shoulders, I could tell that they were crestfallen.

I strained forward, stood on tiptoe, attempting to glimpse the vital orders. Shoulders and heads kept getting in the way. "Bomber school!" someone exclaimed upon reading his name. "That's not so bad. I was afraid I'd be a mechanic!" One by one the men read their names and assignments, then wandered off, alone or in groups, some loquacious, others silent.

"Hey, Kuwahara!" Oka bellowed, "I made it!" Someone got in Oka's way as he hastened toward me. Unceremoniously, Oka shoved him aside. "Hey, Kuwahara—Yasuo, I made it!"

"Wonderful!" I was genuinely happy, but my nerves were balancing on a razor's edge.

"I looked for your name," he told me, "but they wouldn't give me time—just kept shoving like a bunch of damn cattle. There's Sakamoto up there. Quick, ask him to check your name. Hey, Sakamoto, check Kuwahara's name!" Sakamoto turned back to the board reluctantly, and was crowded aside.

"I think it's signal," he said, "same as me."

"What?" I gasped. Never, not even in the guardhouse had

I experienced such a cold feeling. Nearly choking, I lunged forward, crashing into the back before me.

"Take it easy, Kuwahara, you made fighter pilot all right. Don't knock everybody down." It was Tanaka, and for the first time that grin was gone. He turned away and wandered off.

How did he know I'd made fighter school? Sakamoto had said . . . At last I was standing before the board. Feverishly I went across the list of names. Where was it? I couldn't find it! Where? There it was: "Kuwahara . . . Fighter School"! I turned to go, then looked back once more to make certain. Yes, yes, Sakamoto had been wrong. "Oka!" I held up my thumb. Yamamoto was there with him, both of them beaming. Those two were irrepressible. "Yamamoto, you too!" I laughed. He nodded and we fell upon each other like brothers. "What about Nakamura?" Suddenly I was scared.

"He's in," Yamamoto said, "I read his name."

"Where is he, anyway?" Oka wondered.

Moments later we spotted Nakamura, pushing forward on the outer fringe of the crowd, neck extended, eyes worried. "Hey, fighter pilot!" Yamamoto yelled. "What are you doing over there with all the mechanics?" Nakamura turned, half-smiling. Vigorously Yamamoto motioned to him.

"Come on!" *Yai!*—come over here!" Oka and I joined in the beckoning motions.

"Did you read my name?"

"*Un,*" Yamamoto replied, "you're fighter pilot—with the rest of us, you and Yasbei!"

Yasbei was the name of a famous *samurai*—I beamed under the spontaneous compliment. We tendered our congratulations by slapping Nakamura so violently on the back that he staggered. None of us had ever been so happy—not in our entire lives. For me, this was even better than winning the glider championship.

Approximately a third of the men had been picked for fighter school—far more than we had expected. We four, however, were the only ones chosen from our section at the barracks, and our exuberant joy was dampened when we realized what a difficult time the rest of the men were having.

That night, the night before graduation, many of them sat forlorn in the barrack, brooding. Somehow I felt very sorry for Tanaka. At last his grin was gone. A lot of us had expected him to become a fighter pilot, and we were all mystified. I honestly felt like saying something to him—at least some word of consolation—but I feared he might take offense. And, of course, his chances of becoming a bomber pilot were good.

Moriyama, Shimada, and two or three others were to become mechanics. They were sitting together glumly. Clapping my hands on their shoulders, I said, "Don't feel too bad, my friends. From what I've been hearing, mechanic school is not bad at all. As a matter of fact, it's supposed to be quite interesting." They merely looked at me blankly, and I realized how clumsy I had been. "Anyway," I said, "you'll all probably have a chance to become fighter pilots later on." I didn't really believe my own words, but suddenly found myself in an awkward position. It was embarrassing. Not one of them said a word. Moriyama shrugged and made more of a sneer than a smile. The atmosphere was unpleasant, and I realized that with each remark I was getting in deeper— growing more offensive. "Well . . ." I said, then gave Moriyama a feeble pat, and walked away. Even that made me feel stupid.

The rest of that evening I stayed away from them. When Oka became too boisterous, I cautioned him to be silent. The four of us left the barrack and sat together, staring at the red light out on the control tower. Together we soon forgot the plight of our comrades and began to talk of the future.

I remember well the commanding officer's graduation speech the following day. I had good reason to like the man, and was prepared to feel another glow of patriotism and dedication similar to what I had experienced at the end of basic. This time it was a little different, however, and I remember that speech for another reason. In conclusion he said, "Our future continually grows more serious. It is for you, Nippon's sons, to dedicate your lives—to die valiantly for the cause." We were startled, for this was out of character. For the past half year we had all been so steeped in our own training, we had lost touch with the world around us. It struck me like a cup of cold water in the face that we were at war . . . and this was the very first time I had heard anyone in authority admit the seriousness of Japan's situation.

It was October of '44, and a lot had happened since I'd left home in February. I was not the only one who had undergone a transition. Kwajalein, the first Japanese territory, had been invaded in February, and the Marianas had fallen in June. By July Tojo had openly admitted our loss in the "great disaster" of Saipan and had been relieved as chief of the general staff. His entire cabinet had resigned at the same time. Still, at graduation time, most of us were oblivious of the rapid turn of the war. In a sense the war was real, but in the main it was remote. I had been selected for fighter training—that was the important thing.

Part Four

14

THE FIRST HUMAN BOMBS

Life again changed abruptly. With fighter training before us we were accorded greater courtesy. The tremendous load of punishment had been lifted and our lives were now dedicated to the air. During the first two months we flew training planes similar to regular fighters, though not nearly so powerful and maneuverable, with only one small-caliber gun on each wing. This was our preparation for the advanced Hayabusa 2, the best army fighter then in production.

The course was stringent, involving gunnery, formation flying, air maneuvers and suicide practice. The latter entailed diving at the control tower from specified heights, and was the most difficult part of flying because of the psychological effect—the idea that we were practicing to die. It was taken for granted that any pilot with a disabled plane would die in true *samurai* tradition provided he couldn't make it back to home territory. He would dive into an enemy ship or plane, taking as many of his adversaries with him as possible.

It was with this thought in mind that I made my first plunges toward the control tower. From two thousand feet I looked down at Hiro and the surrounding countryside—ridges and dales a darkening green—farm land stretching out to where the sea sparkled. There was the strip, a cement patch on the earth's surface, planes and hangars lining one end. The trainers were droning along in a series of three-man V's, rising in tiers. I watched as the instructor peeled off and began his dive. The man behind him angled slightly and winged over, following, then the third. They were fading toward the earth. Next formation. Down they went, growing smaller. Next formation.

Just one man ahead of me now. My turn. Easing the stick over left, I felt the earth tip toward me. The first formation was pulling out, then the second, then the first man ahead of me—the earth rushing up, the field and the buildings growing magically.

For an instant I was almost hypnotized. Bigger and closer, bigger and closer—everything! There was the control tower—closer, closer. I was amazed at my own daring. Now! Stick back—the blood in my head surged as though straining to continue its straight downward course. Black splotches were coming at me through the cockpit. I was moving along on the level, still over two hundred feet above the target. Dismayed, I followed the man ahead of me, climbing. It had seemed to me that I was pulling out with only a few feet to spare.

We circled, lifting, preparing for a repeat performance. Moments later I was slicing downward once more. This time! This time I would astound everyone on the field. I wouldn't allow the rising earth to hypnotize me—not this time. I concentrated on the plane ahead, watched it pulling out, and felt disdain. He had pulled out high above the tower. For some reason, however, a moment after he began to level, I envisioned that same plane continuing its straight downward plunge, never pulling out. I could almost see the flames and hear the sound.

Unnerved, I pulled out higher than before. I was irritated at myself, irritated for what I had done, irritated because my hands were unsteady. For a brief flash I had almost known what it would be like . . . what it would be like to keep right on going.

Again and again we repeated our suicide runs, but that day not one man pulled out with any less than two hundred feet to spare. As the days passed, it began to be easier. Occasionally the feeling of death came so strongly that I became unsteady. Once I completed a pass and found myself buzzing along, still at three hundred feet. Deeply chagrined, I cut the distance by two thirds on the next dive.

Gradually we became more confident. We also dived at the outlines of ships and carriers, painted on one end of the strip, and after a few weeks were pulling out with only sixty feet to spare. By now we had developed a sixth sense—something that enabled us to feel, as well as see, how close we were to the ground. Within three weeks our instructors added an innovation. We were to complete the dive with our eyes closed. Dropping from approximately six thousand feet we would count to ten before pulling back on the stick. From half that height we would count to six.

On the first few dives I peeked, just barely, but I peeked. When I eventually summoned enough will power to keep my eyelids clamped, I began counting too fast. Eventually, however, all of us became masters at "blind diving." Even without the count we could tell how close we were to the earth, just as a sightless man may sense a wall before him.

Daily we went through mock "dog fights," perfecting our ability at cutting tight circles, barrel-rolling, aileron-rolling, leaf-dropping, executing Immelmanns, chandelles, etc. Each day my confidence increased, for I was going through our practice sessions with few mistakes. My three companions were also proving themselves capable flyers. While both Oka and Yamamoto flew with a bold abandon, Nakamura was more cautious and precise. Still, there was no doubting his courage. His suicide dives were executed perfectly and each time he pulled out at almost exactly the same level, varying only a few feet.

Gradually the dives became less disturbing, more like a game, losing their real significance. Men diving and killing themselves—purposely? Yes, I accepted it in a sense—but only passively, as I might accept occurrences in a novel or a movie. Somehow one believes . . . and yet, such things are remote. Something buried deep in the brain keeps assuring, "This happens only to other people—not you—not the people you know."

And thus, we received quite an awakening in October. That month our first *Tokkotai* (special attack group) struck the enemy, Japan's first real suicide pilots. Within the next ten months over five thousand planes containing one—sometimes two—men each, would follow in their wake.

"A *samurai* lives in such a way that he will always be prepared to die." Every Japanese fighting man knew these words. "We are expendable." "Be resolved that honor is heavier than the mountains and death lighter than a feather." This was all part of a timeless pattern of thinking, an antique religious philosophy, national Shintoism.

The purposeful destruction of thousands of our pilots, however, was initiated in the mind of a Colonel Motoharu Okamura of Tateyama Air Base. His plan was secretly presented to Vice-Admiral Takijiro Onishi, father of the *Tokkotai,* and later approved by the Daihonei.

Okamura believed that suicide pilots could fan the winds of battle in Japan's favor. "I have personally talked to the pilots under my command," he stated, "and am convinced that there will be as many volunteers as are necessary." After some time his proposal was accepted.

In the latter part of October, only a short time after American troops had landed in the Philippines, the *Daihonei* released a memorable communiqué:

"The Shikishima Unit of the *Kamikaze* Special Attack Corps, at 1045 hours on 25 October 1944, succeeded in a surprise attack against the enemy task force, including four aircraft carriers, thirty nautical miles northeast of Suluan, Philippine Islands. Two Special Attack planes plunged together into an enemy carrier, causing great fires and explosions, and probably sinking the warship. A third plane dove into another carrier, setting huge fires. A fourth plane plunged into a cruiser, causing a tremendous explosion which sank the vessel immediately afterward."

It was a young lieutenant, S. G. Yukio Seki, who became the world's first official human bomb when he led the famed *Kamikazes* on Leyte Bay. Seki, who had only been married a short time, was approached by his superiors and asked whether he would accept the honor. For a moment Seki had paused, just long enough to run a hand through his hair. Then he had nodded. The attack was an astonishing success. Although the pilots had been relatively inexperienced, four of the five Zero fighters, each carrying a 550 pound bomb, had struck their target according to escort observers.

While *Tokkotai* was the general designation for all suicide fighters, each attack group went under a different name. *Kamikaze*, however, the first attack corps, named after the "divine storm" which swamped Genghis Khan's invading fleet in the thirteenth century, became the accepted term. *Kamikaze*, the divine storm, represented our entire suicide onslaught, an onslaught inflicting the heaviest losses in the history of the United States navy, scoring hundreds of direct hits on her vessels. This included attacks from the *oka* bomb also—a one-man glider launched from a mother plane.

And so, by the end of October 1944, *Kamikaze* had become a rallying cry. Whereas the God of Heaven had once hurled the raging elements at our enemies, he would now hurl bomb-laden planes. There was no denying our new-found power. Under the continual bombardment of Japanese propaganda agencies, optimism was kindled. Only a minority, an objective few, perimited themselves to wonder whether *Kamikaze* was not a telling indication of Japan's desperate status.

15

HIGH RENDEZVOUS

Although the first air raid on Tokyo had occurred over two years before, and despite increasing attacks on key Japanese positions, it was not until my fighter training that the first bombs hit Hiro.

By now the loss of such vital bases as Indonesia, Burma, and Sumatra had greatly reduced our fuel supply. Already the shortage was severe enough to prevent our engaging the enemy in long air battles, even with our best fighter planes. Radar stations on our main islands warned of enemy approach. If their course was from Nagoya to the east or Oita, the opposite direction, we relaxed. If they headed for Osaka, between, we took to the sky, fearing they might veer toward Hiro. It was mainly a matter of preserving our aircraft as best we could.

It was just after noon mess one day in November when Hiro's air raid sirens shrieked for the first time in earnest. We rushed to our trainers, thundered down the runway, and headed into the clouds. When we returned, nothing had happened. A flight of fighter-escorted B-29's had by-passed Hiro and assaulted Kure. For several days the same thing occurred. The sirens sounded and we took to the air. Each time we returned to find Hiro unharmed.

Our training was stepped up and soon I was flying the Hayabusa 2. I was a full-fledged fighter pilot now—something I had dreamed of for most of my life. Our furtive hide-and-seek routine with the enemy, however, had disillusioned me terribly. Yasuo Kuwahara was not the invincible *samurai* of the skies, not the glorious fighter pilot who would perform stunts over Tokyo on the emperor's birthday, or on National Foundation Day. No, I was compelled to hide.

The situation filled us with intense disgust. At the same

103

time it was depressing and alarming to realize that our country was in such dire straits. True, we were informed that our runaway role was only temporary, that Japan was prepared for continual enemy encroachments, but somehow such propaganda was losing much of its impact for many of us. Even *Kamikaze* was not really stopping the enemy—not yet.

One day we returned from the clouds to find Hiro belching smoke, one of its hangars ablaze. Half a dozen Liberator bombers had slashed the base, tearing up part of the strip, setting the hangar in flames and destroying part of the fighter assembly plant.

Fire fighters were battling frantically, while a repair crew hastily covered over torn areas along the airstrip. It was some time before we could land, a bitter and dejected group of fighter pilots. After having made our reports in the orderly room, we wandered about the base surveying the damage. Nakamura and I walked slowly along the gray-white runway. I stared at its wounds, amazed that we had been able to land at all. So this was what bombs could do to a base. Neither of us spoke. We simply wandered about, surveying the damage, detached at times, occasionally infuriated. As we stared at the charred hanger, with its wrecked planes, Nakamura muttered, "Fighter pilots that can't fight. Ha!"

Later in the day I visited Tatsuno. He had made his solo flight in the Akatombo and was doing well thus far. With bombs now striking Hiro, it was questionable whether the men would serve a full air apprenticeship. "You'll probably be flying the Hayabusa any day now," I suggested.

Tatsuno laid an arm around my shoulder. "Maybe it will be just the way we always planned. Yasuo, it seems too good to be true in a way. And yet. . . ." He paused, frowning. I waited, feeling that Tatsuno was going to say something I didn't want to hear. "And yet I never expected things would be like this."

"Like—like what?"

"If we are going to win . . . well, when do we start? The attacks are getting worse all the time. When are they going to stop? If we can't stop them now, how can we expect to stop them a month from now, or half a year from now? What's the secret? What are we waiting for?" Tatsuno's voice was quiet and strained.

"Things get pretty bad for both sides, before a war is ever won," I said.

"Yes, but what are we doing? Are we making it as bad for the Americans? Are we bombing California, New York, Washington?" The words hurt.

I sat for a moment longer, then rose. "I guess I'd better get back to the barracks."

"Do you have to leave already? You haven't been here for two seconds."

"I'd better," I replied. "I've got a lot to do," Once I looked back and saw him watching me. I waved, and he lifted his hand. That was the last we saw of each other for a while.

A few days later five of us were flying along the inland sea between Kure and Iwakuni. From twelve thousand feet I looked down. Clouds were forming at an amazing speed, right before my eyes, wisps falling behind like shredded cotton. Far off beyond the mountains a specter moon hung faint and gray. From time to time I peered down at the sea, an eternal expanse, wrinkled and sparkling. How strange . . . to think that throughout the world men were destroying each other. Slightly ahead and above me was Lieutenant Shimada, a veteran combat fighter. He had been in battle many months before, when our planes had so badly outclassed the American P-39's and P-40's. He had known the taste of victory, and more than one enemy had fallen at his hands. I felt my heart brimming with admiration, admiration for the quiet, slender man. How I longed to be that experienced, that capable. The back of his head, the very line of his shoulders, denoted confidence. Occasionally the head would tilt slightly, or barely turn, permitting the eyes to make their vigilant survey. Even in those motions there was precision and evidence of an inner strength.

The vast reaches of the sky, the water, the land, the waning moon—all denoted serenity. I shifted in my seat. Winter would be soon upon us and, gazing toward a distant shore, I remembered my walks with Tomika. I remembered the mild fishermen at their nets—bare toes in the warm sand, laughter. The laughter of fishermen and their wives was different—not the laughter of the bars or the crowded streets. It was part of nature, the lapping of waves mingled with the cries of sea birds. Had the war changed all this? For a while I wanted to turn toward Onomichi. I would land on a lonesome stretch of shore. The dank fish-shacks would be empty now. I would stand and listen for the haunting laughter.

My earphones crackled: "Enemy, two o'clock low!" I glanced down, saw nothing, then over to Shimada. The lieutenant motioned with his thumb and my eyes followed. This time I saw them—formation after formation—a tremendous swarm of Grumman F6F Hellcats, and they were heading for Hiro!

For a moment I lost my breath. No, this couldn't really be happening—not really! I fumbled with my oxygen mask nervously. It was secure. I was awed, stupefied. The enemy planes were like sesame seeds—too numerous to count. Of course, we wouldn't attack, not five of us. They hadn't spotted us, and I was glad of that. Suddenly I decided that it was better just to fly. Air fights? They could come later, later when we had more experience. I glanced back off my right wing at my friend, Nomoto. I motioned as the lieutenant had done, and he nodded. I opened and closed my hand rapidly, indicating the multitude of planes below. Again he nodded.

Now Shimada was turning. Automatically we responded. Now, still undetected, we were following the Hellcats. Could it be possible that we . . . ? No. Nevertheless I checked my guns. Were they ready to go? Yes. It was good to check; one of these days we'd actually be using them—one of these days, but not, not against that many.

My ears buzzed. No! We were going to attack! What should I do? Suddenly I became frantic. I shoved the throttle ahead, feeling my Hayabusa surge with new power. What should I do now? Already I was forgetting everything I had ever learned. Release gas tank! That was it. Otherwise one bullet could blow me into the next world. Our tanks were hurtling downward, and we were moving up fast. What now? Again I adjusted my mask. Again I checked the guns. Just follow Lieutenant Shimada; that's right. Just follow Lieutenant Shimada. Do everything he does and you'll be all right. Remember how you followed The Mantis? Follow Shimada, only not so close, not so close! Don't tense up! Don't freeze on his tail! Relax, Kuwahara, relax. Your back is like a poker. All right . . . better now. All right . . . Shimada's beginning the dive. Over you go, Kuwahara, over you go. Shimada had peeled off, seeming to lift slightly, stood on his wing tip and dropped off fast, his nose angling toward the enemy. I followed his swift tail. The enemy was growing bigger with every second. The sesame seeds had turned into toy planes, the toy planes into fighters, actual fighters with men inside.

106

It is plain now . . . We are going to strike at the rear of the formation, then fan off rapidly. We will hit and run. Too many for anything else. Still the enemy hasn't seen us. Should I fire? No, wait for the leader. Do everything he does. Why doesn't he shoot? We can shoot now, spray them en masse and drop a dozen. I'm sure we can. Closer . . . closer. Guns rattle. Lieutenant Shimada is ripping out short bursts. Curving orange lines are reaching out from him, reaching out to the enemy.

The Hellcats are rolling away. No doubt in their minds now. Fire, Kuwahara, fire! I haven't even squeezed the trigger. Wildly I blaze away. Wild, prolonged blasts. I'm not hitting anything! A Grumman flips crazily—a marvelous maneuver. No, he's hit, I hit him . . . No, Shimada did it! My own tracers are swallowed again and again by the sky. We flash on by, banking and climbing. The entire tail of the Hellcat formation has disintegrated. Surely we can't have shot them all down. The main enemy formation is far ahead, but where are the others?

Shimada's victim was glimmering against the sun, the wing tips dazzling in its rays. But there was something else . . . It was vomiting black smoke, and flames were flapping, colored streamers along the fuselage.

Fascinated, I watched it going down. Exultation and frustration gripped me at the same time. I had never known it woud be so gratifying to see an enemy destroyed. But why couldn't I have done it? Why couldn't I have cut out one of the Grummans, just one, when the chance was so perfect? I didn't even remember having one in my sights. And then they had scattered like so many wary ducks. We were running away, full throttle, and I'd muffed a perfect chance. At least I had kept in formation—almost unconsciously.

From the corner of my eye, I saw something silver flashing above, off my right wing tip, then another and another—silver fish cutting through the water. For some inexplicable reason I glanced down. Slightly behind, and not far beneath, three Hellcats were keeping pace. Wisely, Shimada signaled to run. The rest of us were green and could do little more than hinder him in combat.

But now it appeared that running would not be enough. The enemy above was closing with terrifying speed. I glanced back to see a single plane trailing at three hundred yards.

Suddenly his wings sparkled. He was shooting. The lieutenant's voice sounded and he cut in a tight left circle, the rest of us following.

The maneuver threw off the planes behind and beneath us, but not the three above. Determined snouts were diving at us from the rear, guns flashing. My heart jolted, and my head and upper body seemed to run empty, leaving my arms numb. Whining, shredding noises. Magic holes were appearing in my windshield. For an excruciating moment I was utterly bewildered. The lieutenant veered off, snapping over into a beautiful roll. I followed, managing to execute a similar maneuver. It worked perfectly. Seconds later I found myself on the enemy's tail.

Now! I had him in my sights! I squeezed off a burst. The tracers arched over the top of his rudder. My stomach knotted. This time! Three bursts, all of them longer than the first. The bullets were going home! It was astonishing that my body would even function. In a way it was as though I were witnessing everything from another sphere. The lethal buzz of motors, the staccato of machine guns, and the blue-white sky all had a dreamlike quality.

Mildly surprised, I watched the Grumman lose altitude, trailing a thin wisp of smoke. Ramming my plane into a steep climb, I glanced back to see the pilot bail out. For an instant that white mushroom brought back memories of The Mantis.

Then I realized that I was no longer with our leader—nor was any of us. Americans and Japanese were scrambled throughout the sky. Just then the nasal words came: "I'm going to crash! The rest of you save yourselves!" The voice was Shimada's. Something like a fireball cut a curved section from the sky beneath. He'd been hit. A dazzling flare below, a violent blast. Not until then had the words fully registered.

Like toys cemented together the two planes fell—an American and a Japanese. Then they separated, crumbling, and the crinkling waters rose to meet the blackened fragments.

I felt a strange vibration. My Hayabusa was trembling like a nervous animal. The smooth prop roar was beginning to sound phlegmy, and I didn't seem to be getting enough oxygen. Tearing off my mask, I dropped down over two thousand feet. Then I glanced at my air speed indicator. It didn't register. The wind was screeching through my new bullet holes. I peered at the fuel gauge—little left. I'd never make it to Hiro.

I took a quick look around. Nothing in sight, nothing anywhere. It was as if the wind had come to sweep things clean. Getting my bearings, I circled and limped toward the island of Kyushu. The enemy's 50-calibers had played more havoc than I had ever dreamed. Even my compass was gone. I knew the direction of the island well enough, however. Shortly it was in sight and I hugged the coast to keep my bearings, heading for Oita Air Base.

No trouble now. Soon the landing strip would be in sight. It wasn't until I was preparing to land that another jolt came. A warning signal from the field. My landing gear wasn't down. I pushed the button hard. No! Frantically I pushed, again and again, but the unpleasant signal kept repeating on the ground.

Circling, I began examining my instruments and after a few seconds spotted the trouble. The connecting wire had been severed. Joining the ends was a simple matter. I pressed the button and the wheels lowered into position. In a few seconds I was braking along the runway. My first air battle was over.

16

HONOR AND A LOST CAUSE

Upon returning to Hiro, I learned that two others of our group had made it to safety. My friend, Shiro Nomoto, had been shot down but had survived with a badly shattered leg. Oka, Yamamoto, Nakamura and I visited him at a hospital in Hiroshima a few days later and were depressed at what we found. Nomoto's leg had been amputated and he had attempted suicide.

Antiseptic odors filled my nostrils as we entered the room, and I began to wish we'd never come. What could we say? How could we comfort him? At the same time, I was rather fascinated.

Nomoto looked wraith-like, propped in his white bed. Only his burning eyes indicated what was going on inside. The blanket lay against his body, and dropped away where the leg should have been.

Embarrassed, we greeted him and received a wan smile. I had brought him some magazines. "Thanks, Kuwahara," he said, "but I couldn't read them."

"Well," I replied, "I'll leave them anyway. You'll feel better in a few days." Nomoto half-shook his head and gasped a colorless laugh. There was a strained silence. The others said nothing, and I grew irritated. Someone had to say something! I spoke, and it was the wrong thing: "We know how you must feel, Nomoto. It's not an easy thing." I gripped his wrist, closed my teeth over my lower lip, and stared at his hand for a moment. As I concentrated on his hands, the words came out of their own accord: "From now on, you will be able to do as you please. You have fulfilled your duty to the emperor. You have been a true *samurai*. You have served your country with honor. Now . . . there will be other things for you to do. Perhaps you will soon be finding a wife —*na?*"

"Yes," he said. "Oh, yes! Maybe I can find a good, strong one, one like an ox, who can carry a cripple on her back."

Knowing full well that silence was best, I blundered on: "I know how you feel, Nomoto, but think of Lieutenant Shimada. He . . ."

Nomoto's eyes blazed, and he almost shouted, "No, you don't know how I feel! Would to God that I had followed Lieutenant Shimada. What good am I now—to anybody? What good?" He turned to cover his face and let out a moan of pain.

Silently cursing myself, I looked at the others. There was no accusation in their glances, merely vacuity. Nakamura shook his head and stared at the floor.

Then Oka, with a slight toss of his head, indicated the door, and we all stood up. We couldn't just walk out though. We couldn't just leave him that way. I laid my hand lightly on his shoulder and said, "We'll be seeing you again soon, Nomoto."

Just then footsteps sounded in the hall. A man and woman entered the room—Nomoto's parents. After we had exchanged introductions, the mother walked to her son, murmuring, and laid her hand on his brow. "Here," Oka volunteered, and slid a chair to her. Thanking him, she sat down, still stroking her son's forehead.

Again there was silence until the woman spoke: "Why must people fight? Why? Why must they hate?" Never had I heard words couched in such incredulity. "Oh, the senselessness, the stupidity of it all! Why can't . . . ?" She stopped, then after a moment continued: "Shiro's father and I . . . we did not rear him to be a cripple . . . nor did we rear his brother, Joji, to die. Joji died at Guadalcanal."

When I informed her that I had recommended her son for a medal, she replied, "You are very kind, but what good will a medal be? Will it restore his leg? Will it teach him to walk? Will it return his dead brother?"

I leaned forward, my elbows on my knees, staring out across Hiroshima. How fortunate it would have been if I had only remained at the base. Everything I had attempted in that white room, everything, had been wrong. Why couldn't I vanish? I hated the place—everything it stood for. Better to die any day. Nomoto had been right.

"I didn't mean to hurt your feelings," her voice came. "Look at me." My gaze lifted. "Look at me, all of you," she commanded. We obeyed. Something remarkable about that face. It was compassionate, yet stern. Lined and drawn now, but still captivating. It had been beautiful once. We could not avert our eyes. The woman stirred us with a mixture of feelings.

She spoke to us as a mother: "Listen to me, my sons. Your minds are filled with ideas, ideas of honor, of glory. You think about courage, about dying valiantly—all those things. Why? Why don't you forget about honor and glory? Only seek to preserve your own lives. There is nothing honorable in dying for a lost cause!"

I expected her husband to rebuke her, but he said nothing. Reading my thoughts, she eyed him sharply. "Fathers feel no differently about this than mothers, not deep down inside."

I remembered the way my own father had looked into my eyes and said, "Do you know my heart?"

It was time to go, but all the way back to Hiro I kept hearing those words: "There is nothing honorable in dying for a lost cause." A lost cause! An indescribable feeling crept over me, and I almost shuddered. Throughout that day those words haunted me, and gradually I became indignant. Who was that woman that she could presume to speak such words? A mere woman! And her husband—he must be a small man indeed.

It was as though *she* controlled *him!* He had scarcely spoken during our visit.

But the indignation left as quickly as it had come, and the cold feeling returned. Tatsuno and I hadn't seen much of each other during the last weeks; both of us were too busy, I thought. Now I was realizing, however, that he made me uncomfortable. He was too much like Nomoto's mother. What was it he had said? Something about what was the secret? What were we waiting for?

As the days passed I kept battling a feeling, a feeling that . . . No! I wouldn't permit myself. Surely the words of that woman did not symbolize the attitude of the people at large! But yes, something was lacking; there was no denying it. True, the propaganda still poured down, the same deluge, but it was losing its impact. Certain facts were evident to military men, and how could these facts help seeping through to the people?

For a moment I faced those facts. Japan had been driven back three thousand miles across the Pacific. MacArthur had entered Luzon, vanquishing our forces at Leyte Gulf, and, although I didn't know it then, it was this triumph that virtually eliminated Japan as a strong naval power. Although I struggled to be optimistic, I knew that the loss had devastated combat troop morale. For a long time the Americans had taken very, very few captives. Now, however, our men were surrendering in sizable numbers.

Of course, there was *Kamikaze*. Their attacks had increased on a grand scale, and there was no denying their effectiveness. For a time, this fanned the sparks of hope, but still . . . would *Kamikaze* really stop the enemy? If so, it would require a far greater number of human bombs. Colonel Okamura's estimate that three hundred suicide planes could alter the battle course was obviously too small, far too small.

Still, I reasoned, there might be hope. If a "divine storm" had saved our country once, once when her plight was desperate, why not again? Wasn't the Imperial Way the right way, the best way for the world? Wasn't Japan destined for a role of leadership? If there was a God, one of truth and justice, wasn't it only logical that He could come to our aid? Maybe this was the test. Maybe just when our plight looked blackest. . . .

How many human bombs would it take? There were many who would eagerly give their lives. To many suicide was no sacrifice. But within many others apprehension was growing. As the "divine storm" increased, more and more of us would be drawn into it. It was only a matter of time. The clouds were mounting above Hiro, and the first windy gusts were coming.

17

DEATH GREETS THE NEW YEAR

On New Year's day, 1945, fighter pilots from Hiro's Fourth Squadron held a testimonial ceremony for those of their number who had died. Captain Yoshiro Tsubaki, the squadron commander, had delivered an impassioned speech declaring our moral obligation to avenge those deaths. And later we visited Hiro's military shrine. Not many had died yet, from Hiro. All my close friends were still with me. There was a name though, that I couldn't forget: "Shimada, Jiro." For a long while I gazed at his name plate—one of the valiant dead. Again I saw the two planes falling, the Japanese and the American. I thought about the ashes somewhere at sea. "No more New Years for you, Lieutenant "Shimada," I said, and slowly walked away.

What sad attempts we made, our words of "Happy New Year." They fell like clods to the earth. I suppose all of us were thinking of New Year's Day at home, in times past. I recalled with a groan of nostalgia how Tomika and I had run through our home on that same day many years before. Jubilantly we had scattered beans about to drive out the evil spirits.

It was during the afternoon that Captain Tsubaki called another meeting, a stranger one than the first, for it was then that Hiro's first *Kamikaze* were chosen. "Those of you unwilling to give your lives as divine sons of the great Nippon empire will not be required to do so. Those incapable of accepting this honor will raise their hands—now!" To be a suicide pilot—that was the greatest of honors. Everyone said so. But six men had raised their hands during that meeting, men I knew well. They had been afraid enough, or brave

113

enough, to admit what many of us felt. They had chosen life and had been given death. A dubious honor.

Yes, only a few months before, men had volunteered with alacrity. Now many of them had to be compelled or tricked into it—stern evidence that *Kamikaze* was already considered a futile death by many. Daily the Allies were growing stronger. There was no denying it now. More enemy planes, newer and better fighters. The B-29 Superfortresses, grumbling monsters that they were, had begun to clot the heavens, leaving swaths of fire and death. The enemy naval forces were closing in.

I hated to admit it. I fought, but I had to admit it. We were losing. How long, I suddenly wondered, would the Japanese people be able to hide behind their emotional façade? How long would they remain credulous of the propaganda? How many would be true to themselves? Six had been true at Hiro, and they would pay a heavy price. Early in January they left Hiro for final suicide training.

Periodically from then on, men were selected from my squadron, and transferred to Kyushu for final suicide preparations—never to be heard of again.

For nearly a year we had been carefully conditioned to accept death. For thousands of years, really. It was a part of our philosophy. But now, all at once, the black tentacles were reaching out, inexorably taking, taking. With each departure our sense of doom increased.

I had come through more than one air battle now, and had a second enemy plane to my credit. While flying over the inlet between Kure and Tokuyama, six of us had jumped two American fighters, and it had been surprisingly easy. With over two thousand feet altitude on them we veered off and struck before they were aware of us. All six of us opened up simultaneously with cannons and machine guns.

The nearest American literally disintegrated under the combined onslaught and went down in a flaming sheet. The second ran for it, but seemed confused as to whether he should make a beeline, or a sharp arc to throw us off. The result was a curve which both our flight leader and I easily cut inside. In an instant I had him in my range finder, and it was almost that simple. Three or four quick bursts, and he folded, to hit the ocean in a smoking tail spin. How different from my first encounter with the enemy. I felt almost cheated.

Yes, I was becoming a fairly capable pilot, as was Nakamura, for he had one plane to his credit. But no matter how good we might become, no matter how many adversaries we might vanquish, it was only a matter of time. The sense of doom was increasing with each hour.

Only one hope for survival, and that a tenuous wisp which I kept dispersing. It was February and the enemy was attacking Iwo Jima, just 750 miles from our capitol. Perhaps the war might end. More than one man prayed for this—not for the defeat of his country but for a sudden cessation of hostilities. Many of the civilians still had faith, but we who lived close to the facts had to be either naive or fanatical to expect triumph now.

In just a few weeks my awareness of Nippon's pending fate had snowballed. Since surrender seemed inevitable, I prayed for it to come swiftly. How often the woman's words sounded now, even in my dreams: "There is nothing honorable in dying for a lost cause." It was a race against time, and an ironical one, for only the enemy could save me. I almost laughed at the thought.

Some of us did have greater hope than others. On the whole our men at Hiro were inexperienced, and already I was among those rated as top pilots. We would be preserved as long as possible to provide base protection, and the best among us would soon be escorting suicide missions, defending them on the way to their targets, returning with the reports.

Consequently, our poorest pilots died first, causing the Americans to conclude, initially at least, that there were no skillful *Kamikaze*. (The American Admiral Mitscher put it this way: "One thing is certain: there are no experienced *Kamikaze* pilots.")

Regularly orders from the *Daihonei* in Tokyo were sent to key air installations throughout the four main islands, stipulating how many pilots each base would contribute at any given time.

In turn, these centers drew men from bases within their jurisdiction. For example, Hiroshima drew from nearby Hiro, Kure, and Yokoshima Air Bases on the main island of Honshu. Men were then committed to special suicide bases such as Kagoshima, the largest, on the southern inlet of Kyushu.

Generally *Kamikaze* attacks were mounted in waves of fifteen or twenty planes, at thirty-minute intervals. Some of our suicide pilots were allegedly sealed or locked into their cockpits, but I never witnessed such proceedings. As far as I could determine, there was simply no reason for it. Frequently *Kamikaze* opened their canopies and signaled with flags or scarves upon sighting American ships—a final show of bravado, a last booster, which possibly helped some of them to perform that fatal plunge.

No one will ever comprehend the feelings of those men who convenanted with death. Even condemned convicts don't understand it fully. The convict is atoning for misdeeds; justice is meted out. Of course, there have been heroes in every nation, who have deliberately laid down their lives, but where before in all the world has there been such premeditated self-destruction? Where before have thousands of men diligently set about their own annihilation, mulling over all the details for weeks, sometimes months?

Neither the Shintoistic concept of a post-mortal existence as a guardian warrior in the spirit realms nor the Buddhistic philosophy of Nirvana has always provided solace. The "mad, fanatic Jap" was too often a schoolboy, enmeshed in the skein of fate, not above weeping for his mother.

Not that there weren't fanatical Japanese fighters. Some wanted nothing but to die gloriously, to gain revenge. Even the subdued, bespectacled student, browsing through some Tokyo library, might be molded by circumstances into a flaming soul, dedicated to death. And there were a few who seemed to approach doom as though it were no more than a morning stroll.

Generally, however, we pilots moved along two broad paths. The *Kichigai* (madmen) were fierce in their hatred, seeking honor and immortality, living for only one purpose —to die. Many of these came from the navy air force, which contributed a far greater number of *Kamikaze*.

As time passed, I allied myself more closely with a second group, whose sentiments were usually the opposite, though rarely expressed openly. These men, mainly the better-educated, were referred to as *Sukebei* (libertines) by the *Kichigai*. Not that the *Sukebei* were unpatriotic. I would die for my country today if necessary, as I would have died then. But life was decidedly dearer to us. We saw no purpose in death for death's sake.

Naturally there was a middle ground, also, and each man's attitude fluctuated. There were many times when I longed for revenge. Or when I considered that by destroying an American ship I might save many of my people . . . then my own life seemed insignificant.

How often I had struggled for a certain attitude toward death—a special, indescribable feeling. What was it that made men unafraid? Was it courage? What was courage? "We are expendable!" That was the cry. "Be resolved that honor is heavier than the mountains and death lighter than a feather." Countless times I had repeated those words. With some men the feeling was innate. With me it was ephemeral; I was always fighting to re-kindle the flame.

My friends were still with me, Tatsuno now a full-fledged fighter pilot. To be a fighter pilot, to be with my friends, that was what I had always dreamed of. But how long would it last? Some of us were bound to go soon, no matter how good we were. Which one of us would be taken first?

Daily I went through our routine suicide practice. Methodically I performed each dive—with perfection now but with little satisfaction. Mechanically I went through the exercise, beginning with a cold feeling in the stomach, which always expanded into a dread. More than once the words came: "Go on! Keep right on going! Crash! Smash yourself! End it! No more fear, no more sorrow." Then I would pull out, calling myself a coward.

There were occasional air battles, most of them only quick scraps or sorties, in which we hit swiftly and ran. Invariably the enemy outnumbered us, and our lives were to be dedicated to something more important than a mere air skirmish. Japan was like a man dying in the desert, with little water left. The drops had to be used sparingly, saved for the hours when the sun would burn its hottest.

As the months faded, Japan began to stagger, losing her grip on eastern China. The heart of Tokyo had been demolished and the entire homeland was being destroyed. Millions of tons of our merchant shipping had been sunk, and by the emperor's birthday in April of '45, the enemy was assaulting Okinawa, Japan's very doorway.

This was a crucial time. Premier Suzuki had told the Japanese cabinet, "Our hopes to win the war are anchored solely in the fighting on Okinawa. The fate of the nation and its people depends on the outcome." Okinawa fell. Eighty-one days of violent battle.

The months writhed by, and one day in May it happened . . . Oka and Yamamoto. I had returned from a flight over

117

western Shikoku, and learned the news. I hadn't seen either of them for two or three days. We'd been flying different shifts, doing reconnaissance. And now it had come . . . what I had been fearing all along, but never really expected. Orders had come down suddenly, and my friends had been transferred to Kagoshima. Oka and Yamamoto, gone! I couldn't believe it. I rushed to their billet. Surely they couldn't have been taken so quickly!

The door creaked as I entered, and I looked down the line of cots. The bedding was gone from two of them, the mattresses rolled, exposing the barren springs. There was something horrible about those beds; the naked springs cried out. I opened my dead comrades' lockers and listened to the hollow clang, a death knell.

Dazed, I sat down on one of the empty cots, feeling the springs sag. It was as though Oka and Yamamoto had been carried off by a sudden wind. How could such a thing have happened? No time, no notice, I was alone in the billet, and for a while there was nothing but silence, not even the sound of motors. For a long time I stared at the far wall, on through it. I saw nothing, felt nothing. It was too much to think about. The place was so empty! The barrack was a murky void.

No telling how long I sat there, insensible. Eventually I was conscious that a hand rested on my shoulder. Nakamura. I hadn't heard him enter. Without speaking, we looked at each other. Someone was with him. Tatsuno. I extended my arm and he gripped it.

"You know," I said at last, my voice dry, "I had the strangest feeling while I was sitting here. It was just as if . . ." My voice cracked. "It was just as if everybody had left. This whole base was empty—nobody, nobody anywhere. It was weird. Have you ever had that feeling?"

"They said to tell you good-by, Yasbei," Nakamura said. (My friends were always calling me after the *samurai* now.) "Still joking, even when they got into the truck." Nakamura gave a half-laugh. "You know what that Oka said—his last words? He said, 'You and Yasbei take good care of all our *musume* (girls) in Hiro!' "

I gave a wry laugh myself. Neither of us, or Tatsuno for that matter, ever went to Hiro, or the nearby cities. We rarely drank, and knew little of the city women with whom our extrovert friends had associated.

118

For an instant I recalled my times with those two, remembered when we first really got acquainted that winter night so long ago, when I'd found the warm shower. They'd been joking then. Even in combat they joked. They were two of a kind, always together. Ironically they had gone together.

"Always the jokers," I mused, "even . . ." I stared at my two friends. "But why did they go so soon? Good pilots! Both of them!"

"Yes, pretty good," Nakamura admitted, "but lone wolves, maybe a little erratic. The days of the lone wolves are gone."

"I know, Nakamura," I said, "but look at some of the pilots in this squadron—not half as good, not half as good!"

"Maybe they're putting the names in a hat now," Tatsuno suggested. "That way it's more interesting. That way, you don't know whether it will come in five minutes or a year."

"Let's get out of here," I said. "Let's take a walk—anything."

Part Five

18

WIND AMONG THE LANTERNS

Sometimes *Kamikaze* didn't seem so terrifying. After all, there were many ways one could die. The bombs were coming continually now, and we were learning what it was like to scramble like rats for our holes. Sometimes the enemy would sneak through our radar screens, and the alarms would scream with scant notice. Now we knew what it was to feel the ground shudder with explosions, to cower in dust-choked craters, while the slower men were blown apart. Once I had seen two laborers running, the bombs dropping right on top of them. I had closed my eyes, then opened them. Nothing left but new craters.

Regularly now, the hangars and assembly plant were being strafed and dive-bombed by Hellcats, P-51 Mustangs, and light bombers.

Then one fatal day in June, a hundred and fifty B-29's pulverized Hiro and nearby Kure Navy Port. The warning had sounded thirty minutes beforehand and, aware of their numbers, every available pilot had taken off to preserve our remaining aircraft. But after that bombing there was no Hiro, no base to which we could return. We flew all the way to Oita Air Base in northeastern Kyushu.

It was at Oita that I became a suicide escort. Today only a few of us are alive—the only ones who can testify to what really happened out there with the American ships, testify to how the doomed pilots acted and felt at that final moment.

Life at this base became increasingly grim, but even so it was fascinating to note individual reactions. The physical punishment of earlier days was gone. Tested and proved, we were among the cream of the army's fighting airmen. As such we were provided with extra money and told to have a good time during off-hours. Men who had rarely touched liquor took to heavy drinking, and many of them who had never even kissed a woman joined the long lines before the prostitute's door—ten minutes a turn.

Women and drink had long been considered vices as far as fighter pilots were concerned—not exactly immoral as Westerners might interpret it, but wrong because fighter pilots had a duty to perform, a vital obligation which nothing should hinder.

In our own case, however, greater license was granted. We were the men with numbered days, and everywhere the sense of finality was growing. People who would have condemned others for such actions said nothing. Life was short, and the airmen were highly esteemed, almost idolized by the public.

To some, religion and a pure life became all the more meaningful. There were those of us who went into the mountains to feel the restful hand of nature, to meditate. Often Nakamura, Tatsuno and I would go off together; sometimes we tried to forget the serious aspects of life as completely as it was humanly possible to do. Other times we sat and conversed a bit portentously for our age. Tatsuno was the real philosopher, though, always seeing deeper into life's mysteries than most people.

Despite all he had seen of death and sorrow, Tatsuno believed that man had a purpose, that life, no matter how trying, was all a test, that even the most terrible physical or mental pain had a place in man's eternal picture.

Once the three of us sat on a knoll, gazing across the shore line to the horizon where evening clouds were forming feathers of pink. "Some day," Tatsuno mused, "all this sorrow will be important only according to how we have met it. I mean . . . take a thing like pain. Some men seem to come away from it all the stronger. Or take death. Some men see it, and . . . well, they seem to gain a greater appreciation for all the things of life, a greater reverence, maybe. It's . . . it's just as if the spirit inside had been polished a little more. I can't help feeling that this is all that will really count some day."

Then there were those times when I took solitary walks, when my friends had other things to do. Alone, one Sunday morning, I wandered past small, well-tended farms, toward the mountains. On either side of me were the rice fields, dotted at intervals with farmers, some with yokes over their shoulders, carrying "honey buckets" of human dung, others irrigating and working the soil with hoes. Those farmers were crafts-men, their crops laid out with drawing-board precision.

In the fields old women were weeding. For hours they would bend in the traditional squatting position, nothing visible but their backs, and umbrella-sized straw hats.

These aged, brown women of the soil lived to work. For them work was more than expediency. It was life itself. They had known hardship. Many had lost sons in the war. Many had been forced to sell their daughters. But always those weathered faces were ready to form cracked smiles. For them, life was amid the rice, where the sun warmed their backs, and the mud oozed up between their toes. Another woman nearby sometimes with whom to share soft conversation, easy laugh-ter. That was life, and it was enough.

Never before had I envied old women. I moved up the dirt road, passing an ox with a ring in his nose. He was tied to a tree, switching his inadequate tail at the flies. The ox didn't seem to mind much. That was his life, there beneath the tree. The hole in his nose had formed a scarred lining long ago, and the ring didn't hurt now. Take out that ring, and he might wander vaguely. Probably, though, he'd stay where he was, just flicking his tail. That was good enough. The situation didn't matter so much. Acceptance, resignation —that was the important thing.

At the foot of the mountain the lane fanned into a broad, graveled road, extending a hundred yards to a stone stair-way. The steps ascended in tiers, passing beneath great, wood-en archways. Midway, a woman with a yellow parasol was carrying a baby on her back—the only people in sight.

For an instant I felt lonely. I wanted to walk with that woman. We wouldn't have to talk, not if I could just feel her presence. It would be good to look at that baby, strapped to her back. He wouldn't be dangling limply, I knew. He would be hugging that back like some tiny, arboreal creature, his bright eyes shining over her shoulder.

Passing through the upper arch, I emerged in a clearing, where temples and shrines lay in a half-moon with their curving eaves and intricately carved walls. Part of one façade was carved with golden dragons, another with lions possessing almost human faces. Still another was adorned with flying ducks and flowers. At the entrance to the clearing an aged man and a girl, perhaps his granddaughter, were selling am-ulets. All alone, those two—just the old man and the little girl—where sun and trees laced the land with light and shadow, where a breeze played along the lattices and the aged buildings.

Having brought one of the charms, I walked forward toward the buildings. At the entrance to the main temple were many lanterns, the center one—red, black and gold—as big around as a table. I was surprised that so few people were present. But then this was a remote area, and it was still early. Once I glimpsed the yellow parasol, passing among some trees before vanishing behind a pagoda.

I climbed the temple steps, and looked within. There was something about those hallowed confines . . . burnished floors and dark corridors steeped in quietude, faintly echoing the bygone ages. They seemed expectant, as though they had waited a long time. I removed my shoes and entered.

It was cool inside, and I knelt before the great, rounding Buddha. What a peaceful countenance! Almost . . . well, a little smug, because all his problems were solved. For perhaps an hour I sat with my legs tucked beneath me, meditating. I didn't comprehend all the differences between the religion of Buddha and national Shintoism. I knew the simple distinctions well enough, but some of the deeper meanings were muddled in my sixteen-year-old mind. I selected and clung to those concepts of afterlife which best satisfied my changing needs.

But for the moment differences in theology didn't matter. For the moment I was in another world. "If death is anything like this," I thought, "then perhaps it won't matter. No matter how death comes, it is inevitable—a few years one way or the other—it will come just as surely as cherry blossoms fall on the hillside. Then, after that . . . there would be something. There had to be.

Something about that temple impelled me to stay on and on. For there in that sanctuary I was safe. The world beyond the mountain was unreal. I would stay here forever where nothing would ever come to harm. Perhaps I could become a priest. The antiquity, the sacredness, tied the past with the future, and I was at one with eternal things, part of time and the land. Perhaps I would . . . Yes, that's how life was for a priest.

Eventually I rose and walked out into the day. Sitting on the steps was a man in a robe, his head shaven. With his chin resting in his hand, he appeared to be contemplating the trees beyond the clearing. I wondered if I should speak, then thought better of it. Kinder not to disturb his thoughts.

As I walked by, his voice came warmly: "Good morning, airman! You are from Oita?"

"Yes, revered sir," I replied, "I am." Unsure what to say, I paused. "I came up here to . . . It is very beautiful here. I find it very pleasant."

"Where are you going? Are you in a hurry to get somewhere?"

"No, honorable sir, no hurry. This is my day off."

"Then why not sit with me a moment? We will appreciate the trees and the clouds together."

Bowing, I introduced myself. There had been times when I felt uneasy or embarrassed before strangers, especially my elders, but not now. Now, in this late season, it was foolish to be hesitant or timid. It was good to sit in the silence, to feel his presence.

After a time he began to ask me questions: where my home was, how long I had been a pilot, and at last: "What are you doing now?"

"Fighter pilot," I answered. "In a few days I will be flying escort missions."

"For special attack groups," he nodded knowingly.

We talked for several minutes, and all the while I wondered when he was going to speak to me officially, with formality—as a Buddhist priest and as my elder. He never did.

From time to time I watched his profile as we talked, almost like my father's. Once his hand rested on my back. I felt no uneasiness. He could leave his hand there as long as he wanted to. We were friends. A breeze played over us, rustling the lanterns.

"Wind is a strange thing, isn't it?" he said. "We don't know exactly where it comes from. We can't see it. But it is always present somewhere, always making itself felt, always moving. It is one of those things, I suppose, that will always be." He waited. "Do you believe that the spirit of man might be something like that?"

I didn't answer.

"You and I," he said. "I mean that something which makes you *you*, which makes me *me*—it will always be, like the wind. It will always be somewhere moving, doing things."

"I have a friend who feels that way," I said. "I, I want to believe it."

He looked at me. "There is not one thing that ever turns to nothing, you know, not even the physical body. Changed, yes, but not obliterated. Matter, energy—they have always existed. They weren't woven from any empty spool. The most any man, or any thing, can do to them is change them. You cannot take something from nothing, and you cannot reduce something to nothing. Am I right?"

I nodded.

"How then can the essence that makes you *you*—Airman Kuwahara—ever be destroyed, reduced to an utter absence, to nothing? No, you see, my friend, the spirit can leave the body, just as it can enter the body, as it can move the body. But why should that really make us sad? Why should it bother us very much, just so long as we continue? The wind has left these lanterns now. Now it is passing up over the mountain among the trees."

When I rose to go, he said, "Come back again."

"I want to," I replied.

I left the clearing, and descended the long stone stairway, passing beneath the arches.

19

THE MIRACLE OF LIFE

For a day or two I viewed the world a bit differently. My hours amid the farms and mountains always had a pacifying effect. I had accepted the priest's personal philosophy hungrily, and it had appealed to my sense of reason. It had helped, as it always will help.

Even so, no philosophy, no matter how appealing, could pacify what I began to feel after my first escort flight over Okinawa. No air battle had ever left me feeling like that. Never had I seen men purposely plunge to their deaths, one after another.

All during the night after that first flight, I tossed in a near delirium. Endlessly the same pictures flashed through my mind. At times I was accompanying fifteen *Kamikaze*, watching their lives end. At times I was alone, with nothing but boundless water below me. As long as I could see nothing but the water it wasn't quite so bad—except for the loneliness. But it was impossible to keep that water empty for very long. No matter how tightly I clenched my eyes, it was impossible to squeeze out the vision of that first ship, then another and another and another. . . .

All during the night I kept seeing that sinister convoy. The screeching dive—down, down, down—the ships growing—the tracers like red, ruled lines—the flak, blossoming death. Always upon reaching this point, I would leave the nightmare with a jolt. It was the falling sensation every one has experienced, but greatly intensified. Then I lay shuddering, afraid to stay awake, afraid to sleep.

During that night, and in the days to come, I found myself wondering what might become of my body. What an odd sight my head would make, severed by the blast, a charred thing sinking in the ocean. How deep would it sink—a mile, two miles? How deep was the water off Okinawa? I saw a leg tossing on the waves, awaiting a shark, perhaps. And my fingers? Would my fingers seem strange to some fish? Maybe a round eye would stare at something lodged in the seaweed, and then the fish might nibble.

On more than one of those sultry nights my mattress became so damp and hot that I arose and stood by the window, hoping for the faintest whisper of air. I would stand long enough to let the mattress cool a little. Sometimes I turned it over, for the under side was not so hot. For days my chest was covered with heat rash.

During the slightest interlude of relative comfort, I tried to think of home. I didn't write letters as often now, because they were being censored, and some of them had never even arrived. It was mainly a matter of penning trite words I didn't feel—no satisfaction.

Even so, both mother or Tomika wrote me faithfully. Onomichi had been bombed, but none of my family or neighbors had been hurt, they said. Now, after so many months away, certain memories were temporarily blotted out. Everything about Onomichi was a dream. No, I didn't think about home so often any more.

Now that I was an escort, Nakamura, Tatsuno and I didn't see each other so often, and our barracks were some distance apart. Sometimes Nakamura and I flew the same missions, but

Tatsuno, with less experience, was only flying reconnaissance and furnishing base protection.

Despite it all, though—the anguish, fear, horror, fleeting hopes, frustration—we escort pilots were learning something valuable. we were learning what was required for a *Kamikaze* to die effectively, once the convoy was sighted.

By watching others go, I was gaining experience, and many times daily I planned and rehearsed my own death attack. Mine would at least be a successful one. I knew the best way, from having watched too many failures. I would take a lot of the enemy with me!

To a novice it might seem a simple matter to dive into a ship. However, there were factors which made it extremely difficult. There were the ever-vigilant enemy fighters. In addition, each vessel threw up an astounding barrage. The combined output of anti-aircraft cannons, rockets and heavy-caliber machine guns created a lead wall. Then, too, the ships often zigzagged, so that a plane coming straight down might find only a patch of water awaiting him. Often during predawn attacks it was easy to become confused. One *Kamikaze*, from another base, was reported to have mistaken a tiny island for a ship during the dawn attack. A billowing eruption against the gloomy shore had evidenced his error.

In my own estimation, the best procedure was to descend anywhere from ten to five thousand feet, the sun at our tails. The dive varied from forty-five to sixty degrees, leveling out at about five hundred yards from the target, striking for the stern as low to the water as possible.

Thus an approach was effected below the angle of the bigger guns. It was advantageous for another reason: that way ships were in danger of hitting each other with their own ammunition.

Despite our most desperate efforts, however, the average number of hits was only ten to fifteen per cent—a sad contrast to the first results at Luzon.

20

WOMEN OF THE SHADOWS

Unlike so many of my associates, during all my months in the air force I had spent little time in the cities. Rarely did I enter the bars, and never once patronized any of the innumerable brothels. Because of this, as any military man may surmise, I received a lot of good-natured teasing. It is not easy to explain why I—and a relatively few others, including Tatsuno and Nakamura—abstained. For, as I have intimated, sexual relations out of wedlock are viewed by the Japanese a bit differently than they are by people of a good many other cultures. The satisfying of physical appetites need not be immoral, it is thought, so long as it does not interfere with one's duties and obligations.

My own attitude was partly the result of pride. Having come from a rich family of high social standing, I would not readily debase myself by association with some of the low city life. My outlook also resulted from the fact that I was young, that women made me uneasy. It was even hard for me to talk with women outside my own family.

In any event, I didn't consider the purchasing of sex, like beef across the counter, especially admirable. Certainly it was no achievement. One man's money was as good as another's. Too often men, whom the average woman would never have glanced at in civilian life, began regarding themselves as dashing Lotharios.

Not that I didn't suffer temptation. Sometimes at night, outside the base, I heard feminine voices, laughter—sometimes warm and comforting, sometimes brazen and seductive. Often those sounds rent me with frustration. "The time is late, Kuwahara," I would tell myself. "Better live life to the fullest. Go find the best in town. You've got the money."

More than once I recalled, on a walk through the city with Tatsuno and Nakamura, the different streetwalkers who approached us. One in particular—a woman, perhaps in her early thirties, with large, jutting breasts and a painted mouth. She had seized my arm and tugged me toward a shadowed doorway. I remembered the throaty voice: "Come on, young airman. I can make you happy all night long—only a few *yen!"*

Simultaneously excited and disgusted, I had shaken her off, saying, "No, no, thank you." How Tatsuno and Nakamura had laughed.

Then they had almost roared when in mock anger she called, "Oh, you don't like a good woman! You are not even a man yet, just a baby. Come back when you are a man, *aka-chan;* maybe I will give it to you for free!"

Since we were now allowed overnight passes, only a few men slept in the barracks. On those hot nights I tossed, often talking to myself. I would wipe the sweat from my upper lip and hear the words: "Come back when you are a man, baby dear . . ."

Once, about midnight, I sprang from my cot and began yanking on my clothes, nearly tearing them. Damn that leering face! That smug, brazen . . . Damn that sexy, ogling face! I'd show her! She wouldn't be calling me a baby—not when I was through with her. She'd moan! She'd weep! She'd plead! That's what she would do.

I stubbed my toe and swore, then blundered into my open locker door and swore even louder. "What's the matter, Kuwahara?" a voice came from the other end of the barrack.

Smothering a desire to shout, "Shut up, and go back to sleep!" I stood by the locker, clenching my fists. For a long time I stared into its confines, letting its darkness fill my head, letting it blot out the faces and lights. I pulled off my trousers and shirt, and carefully hung them up.

It was cooler when I lay down again, and a breeze was actually sweeping through the barrack. I remembered how I had felt, seeing girls, some no older than fourteen standing in the shadows, along the buildings—a lot of them like girls I had gone to school with.

Then, too, I reminded myself that a visit to one of those houses would not be so satisfying anyway. Nakamura had tried it, just once, and had returned to the base sickened and disgusted. In the early hours of morning he had awakened to gaze at the female beside him. The paint had worn off, and the hair was disheveled and ratty, the breath rasping from her open mouth. Nakamura had left swiftly, suddenly aware that he might have contracted gonorrhea.

No, I would never make Nakamura's mistake. There was something I could do, though, to ease the frustration, to make

129

life more bearable. There were clubs in the towns, run by the military, equivalent to American USO clubs. These places had a rather pleasant, homey atmosphere, where one could eat or drink, if he desired. And there were girls to talk or dance with. What was the name, in Oita? The Toki-waya Club, that was it. I would go there. That would help, maybe, and it might take my mind off Okinawa. Perhaps I wouldn't wonder, quite so often, when my death orders were coming.

21

TOYOKO

An evening in June found me sitting at a table in the Toki-waya. My friends had not wanted to come, and I sat alone, idly contemplating my glass of beer. There were other men there from the base, too many, laughing, dancing, some of them drinking quite heavily.

How, I wondered, could they take life so lightly? Most of them weren't pilots, I decided. Otherwise they couldn't be so frivolous. This was not at all what I'd hoped for. The merriment only irritated me. How long had it been now, since I had seen my family? Over a year. Sitting there, staring into that glass of beer, I realized forcibly that I would probably never see them again. I had known this all along, but now it struck with special impact. Why had I ever come here in the first place? I pushed the beer glass away and leaned with my face in my hands.

Several minutes had passed when someone touched me: "Are you ill?" Startled, I looked up. The voice was soft, the expression inquisitive, sensitive, reminiscent of my sister, Tomika. I must have stared, for she repeated, "Are you ill? Is something the matter?"

Momentarily it occurred to me that she couldn't really be interested, not in my problems. She was being paid; it was just part of her job. But there was something about her eyes, so much like Tomika's, possibly a wistful light. I felt myself fidgeting under her gaze and looked down quickly. "No, no, I'm not sick—just sort of thinking."

Forcing a smile, I looked up, then down again quickly. She was still eying me. "Would you dance with me?" she asked.

Shaking my head, still not looking up, I replied, "I'm afraid I'm not any good. I don't even know how, as a matter of fact."

"Would you mind very much if I just sat here for a little while, at your table?"

I glanced at her again and reddened. Still the same expression. She had not once averted her eyes from my face. "Yes," I said, "I mean no, I would be happy to have you, if you want to." We sat in silence, until I summoned enough courage to look at her once more. Her eyes caught mine and held them. Yes, she was much like Tomika, not so much the physical appearance as the expression, the whole manner. I looked at the intricate flowered designs on her *kimono*—silver and gold—and let my glance run down to the soft white *tabi* —stockings with separate "finger" for the big toe.

Her feet looked so neat and delicate in their woven *zori* (sandals). Everything about her was neat and delicate, and yet she possessed those fluid, feminine contours that any man would eye with interest. It was the expression, more than the actual features, which made her almost beautiful. Without the expression, without the special light in the eyes, it would have been—merely a nice face.

Vainly I tried to think of something to say. Conversation with my friends had never been difficult, but now . . . with this woman just looking at me . . . "Well . . ." I said finally, "I suppose I'd better be getting back to the base." Intending to sip my beer, then rise, I lifted the glass and, taking a large gulp, nearly choked.

Then I half-stood, but her hand pressed on my own and she said, "Wait, please!" Mystified, I sat down. Could it be that . . . that she was infatuated with me, perhaps even in love? I'd seen romances a lot like this in the movies—read about a few in books. "Would you mind very much if I asked you a personal question?" she murmured.

"Uh, no, I guess not. No!" I wondered why I had answered so loudly.

"Please don't be offended," she said, "but how old are you?"

So that was it. I felt myself getting angry. Almost gruffly I replied, "I—I'm twenty, why? Why do you ask?"

"*Ah so desuka.* Is that so. Twenty?"

"Yes, I am! Why?"

"Oh, you are angry, aren't you? You see, the reason I asked . . . My younger brother . . . I just had to tell you. You remind me so much of him—so very much. He was killed in Burma." There was a pleading quality in her eyes now—the way Tomika had looked up from my picture album that night I enlisted, many months before.

"Oh, I'm sorry."

"He was only sixteen."

For a long time we looked at each other. I didn't want to leave now, but something compelled me to. She disquieted me. Somehow she had intruded herself into my private life. Sweetly, humbly, yet almost insistently, she had managed to look into my mind. I stood. "I have to get back."

"Sayonara," she smiled. Now she was letting me go too easily.

I hesitated. "I'm sorry about your brother, I really am. I'm . . . I'm only sixteen too."

For the first time she took her eyes off me. Looking down at the table, she nodded the least bit, reached out and once more touched my hand. "Will you be coming back?"

"Yes," I said, "I probably will." Then I left.

The following evening, having flown another escort mission that day, I returned to the Tokiwaya, ordered a beer and sat down at the same table. Minutes passed during which I feigned interest in my beer, in the dancing, in anything that happened around me. But all the while there was only one thought— was she somewhere looking at me? Was she approaching my table now? I sipped my beer, stared appraisingly at the glass, then peered from the corners of my eyes. Each time a girl passed by, my heart squirmed.

An hour passed. I was beginning to fidget. Once I thought I saw her, dancing with an airman I knew. But no, it was someone else.

Another thirty minutes passed, and I stood to go. Bitter, I thought of having to return—another hot, nightmarish night in the barrack. A girl passed by carrying bowls of *soba* noodles. Surprising myself, I attempted to halt her: *"Ano! Pardon me!"*

"What would you like?"

All at once it occurred to me that I didn't even know what name to ask for. "That girl I was with—last night—she was sitting here at this table with me for quite a while. Do you

132

know which one I mean?" She had no idea. Vainly I attempted a description. "The one with the long hair—wears it tied in back—the pretty one."

"I'm sorry," she said, "I haven't been working here long."

I sat a moment longer, brooding, then got up and strode toward the door.

I closed the door behind me, shutting out the music and laughter, and wandered down the street. Maybe a little walk around town. Maybe I would go see a prostitute. That would serve her right—asking me to come back, then not even being there! I spat in the gutter, and heard the clop-clop of *geta* behind me.

"*Ano!*" It was the same girl I had just queried. Breathlessly she accosted me: "The girl you were asking for—it's her night off."

I offered my thanks. Bowing, the girl tittered, "You're welcome."

"Wait," I said as she turned to leave. "What's her name?"

"Toyoko, I think."

Ordinarily I never would have asked the next question, but now I had to. "Where does she live?" The girl hesitated. "I'm supposed to give her an important message," I said lamely.

"I don't know for sure. I couldn't say, for sure."

"You must have some idea." I tried not to sound exasperated. "I'm supposed to tell her something important."

"Well . . ."

I jerked a ten-yen note from my wallet. "Here, just tell me where you *think* she lives. I've got to talk to her!"

"Oh," the girl said, "I wasn't trying to get money."

"Take it," I said. "I know you can use it. Just tell me where you think she lives."

"I think she lives down by the beach—in the Miyazaki apartments."

"Thank you very much," I said, and left her.

"I'm not sure, remember!" Her voice trailed after me.

It took me a while to find the place, but at last I was in front of it. The Miyazaki apartments were fairly small, back behind a false stucco wall with a lattice on top. It wasn't ten o'clock yet, and several of the windows were lighted.

Sliding back the door, I entered the gloomy alcove and peered at the mailboxes. There were only six, two of them without names. The last box had the name: "Toyoko Akimoto." That had to be it. I slipped off my shoes, mounted the stairs and stopped at Room 6. A light was shining from beneath the door. Taking a deep breath, I knocked and waited, fairly burning inside. No answer. I knocked louder. Perhaps she was asleep. Or maybe someone was there with her. I couldn't stand the thought.

Quietly I tried the panel. It caught, then slid open an inch, squeaking softly. Two small rooms, a smaller one raised a foot off the main one, opening onto a tiny balcony in back. "Toyoko," I called softly, "Miss Akimoto." This was all a dream. It was crazy. Someone left one of the downstairs rooms and went out, giving me a start. This was a woman's place, though. It smelled nice—faintly of perfume. Yes, it was a woman's place. There were *kimono* hanging on the wall. One of them was pink, another violet. The only furnishings in the main room were a mahogany-colored coffee table, a charcoal burner, and two cushions. In the back room a single *futon* was laid out for sleeping. Another was folded on top of it, along with two sheets and a nightgown.

Entranced, I opened the door wider. Lying across a tiny, child-size dresser inthe back room was a pair of silk hose —a real rarity. It was surprising how any place could so definitely belong to a woman, and no one else. An easy wind filtered through, swaying the stockings, billowing the curtains off the open balcony. I knew that I should leave. What if the place didn't even belong to her? What excuse could I give, anyway? Yes, I would have to leave. I marveled at my own stupidity. I could no more explain this . . . Except I wanted to see Toyoko's face, see her eyes—have her just touch my hand and say a few words. Why should there be anything wrong with that? Once I turned and nearly started down the stairs. As I did so, a faint tinkling sound drifted to me. It was coming from the balcony. Cocking my head, I edged back to the door. A soft, clinking, silvery sound—a sound that made even the hot night a little cooler. I'd heard that sound before, somewhere in the past. Yes, glass chimes, hanging out on the balcony, with the wind running its fingers through them. I could even see fragments of glass, turning back and forth, reflecting light like miniature stars.

Not caring what happened to me, I remained listening to that enchantment. After many minutes the door opened below. *Geta* clopped against the floor in the alcove—one after another. Then someone was padding up toward me.

Wearing a *yukata*, bent low over the stairs, she failed to

134

notice me until the door was half opened. Then she started, putting her hand to her mouth. I struggled to speak and said nothing. For a moment we stared at each other. She had a towel in her hand, and looked different without her make-up. The luxuriant hair was not tied. It flared clear down her back.

"Oh," she breathed. "It's you. You frightened me."

I opened my mouth to speak and shoved the words out: "I'm sorry. I was just leaving. I didn't mean to . . ."

"No," she said, "it's just that I wasn't expecting you. I mean, I wasn't expecting anybody. I just got back from the bath and . . ."

"I'd better go." I spoke more steadily now. "They told me this was your night off, and, well, I thought I'd better tell you I don't know how soon I'll be coming back to the Tokiwaya. We're flying a lot of missions now." I couldn't think of anything else to say at the moment.

"Oh, no!" she shook her head. Her eyes met mine as on the previous night and her hand reached out. "You aren't going to . . . I mean, this isn't . . . You aren't going, not for good?"

"No," I replied with greater confidence, "not for good—not for a while yet."

"Wait here just a minute, please," she said and slipped inside, closing the door. Soon the door opened. "Come in."

Stupidly I mumbled, "Are you sure it's all right for me to be here?"

She handed me a cushion, saying, "It's much nicer out on the balcony. You can feel the sea breeze and look out on the water." A tiled roof slanted below the balcony, dropping off into a walled garden. I could gaze beyond, down a gentle incline, over lanes, roof tops and trees, to the white-fringed shore. Tilting her head back, half-closing her eyes, she murmured, "Hmmm, I love that. It smells so good!" The wind was quite strong now, rumpling her still-damp hair.

"I like those chimes," I said. "I could listen to them forever. I haven't heard any for a long time—not since before I joined the air force. Where did you get them?"

"They were given to me," she smiled, "by a friend. Look, why don't you take off your socks and dangle your legs over, the way I'm doing?"

"Oh, this way is fine."

"Come on," she insisted, and tugged at my toes, pulling the

135

socks off. While I laughed uncomfortably, she rolled my trouser cuffs a turn. "There, now! Put your feet over. That's the way. Feel the wind? Doesn't that feel a thousand times better?"

"Ee," I smiled, "it really does." In some ways she was like a little girl, natural and unaffected. I was beginning to feel at ease. This hadn't been a mistake after all.

"Last night," I said, "you asked me a question—remember?" Toyoko nodded her head. "May I ask you the same one?"

"Oh, that. I'm twenty-four. I'm an old, old woman."

"You said I reminded you of your brother. That was strange. I was surprised to hear you say such a thing, because just before you said it, I was thinking how much you reminded me of my sister, Tomika."

We talked for nearly two hours, about our pasts. Toyoko had left a large family in Nagasaki when she was eighteen, and had supported herself ever since, working in bars, once as a maid in a mansion. She had traveled for several months with a troop of dancers, modeled for big department stores occasionally, and for the past year had been a hostess at the Tokiwaya.

"It's been good, Yasuo—talking to you," she said as I left. "This is the first night I haven't been lonely in months. Will you come back soon?"

"Yes, yes, any time. I mean, if you want me to."

"Of course I do," she said. "Can you meet me tomorrow night? I'll be off at ten. Maybe we can go for a walk—maybe down along the beach."

That night I returned to the base happier than I had been in a long time. Even the flights loomed less sinister—and the whole future. I felt rays of hope. For the first time in my life I was actually feeling a close kinship with a woman outside my own family. I decided that living with men only, year in, year out, could become quite deadening.

Almost every night during the following week I met Toyoko, and as the days passed I began taking rations from the base to her home. Food of any kind was hard to get now, and it made me happy to help her. When it was impossible to obtain onions for our *sukiyaki,* Toyoko would use cabbage. Even the cabbage was rationed, but she got what she could from the market. With almost a maternal expression she would watch me devour great quantities of her cuisine.

Every few days I brought clothes for her to wash; despite my reluctance, she had insisted. She evidently took delight in doing things for me. Toyoko's apartment had become a home —a sanctuary where we agreed never to talk about the war.

Late one Saturday night when I was ready to return to the base, Toyoko eyed me inquisitively and said, "Yasuo, do you really have to go?"

"It's late," I answered. "I can't keep you up all night."

Her eyes softened. "Stay here. You can stay here; it will be all right." When I mumbled inarticulately, she explained, "I have two *futon*—and two sheets. We can both have one of each. Oh, why not, Yasuo? I'll sleep here, and you can sleep in by the balcony—in where it's cool. Look, we can even draw the curtains." Two white veils attached to a curtain rod could be closed to separate the rooms.

"All right," I said. It took only a minute to lay out the *futon,* and I stretched out in the dark, listening to the whisper of cloth as Toyoko undressed in the next room. The chimes tinkled almost over my head, and off in one of the lanes an itinerant noodle-vendor tweedled his flute.

22

CHIMES IN THE NIGHT

I was staying with Toyoko regularly now, and it was almost as natural as being with my own family. Despite the age difference, we had much in common, and needed little more entertainment than the sound of each other's voices. Sometimes we sat at evening in the rear garden, and leaned against a large rock by the wall. Overhead, like a canopy, curved the flowering branches of a tree—fragrant, red blossoms that fell on us from time to time. Often Toyoko placed a stick of incense in a rusted urn, and we would breath in the odor, while each breeze flirted the smoke into snakes and swirls.

As much as I wanted to be with Tatsuno and Nakamura, I wanted to be with Toyoko more. I had to be with her. Occasionally I wondered how she could be content to spend her free time with one so young as I—such a normal relationship in a way, and yet so strange.

My friends were beginning to make remarks. This was inevitable. More than one flier referred to Toyoko as my "wife," and others began enviously plying me with questions. My reticence only piqued their curiosity. When I returned to the barracks, prior to morning formations, I was always met with: "How was it, Kuwahara?" or, "Hey, lover! How come you never live in the barrack any more?"

Of course most of the men were never aware of my absence, since they were always gone themselves. To those inquisitive few, however, I made little effort to clarify the situation. In the first place, they never would have believed me, and any who might have believed would have ridiculed me mercilessly. Then too, I thought too much of Toyoko to open her private life to the air force.

With Tatsuno and Nakamura it was a different matter. "For your own information," I once told them, "this is not what you think it is."

Nakamura swore. "You mean to tell me that you can go spend the whole night with a *musume* like that and never . . . I mean, not even once?"

"No," I replied, "not even once. Can't you visualize our just being friends? We have supper together, go for walks down on the beach. We talk. We don't even sleep in the same room."

"We believe you," Tatsuno replied. "Don't get so excited. I can see what Yasbei means, though. I'd give anything for a situation like that—really! Just a nice girl to be with, to talk with. Half the guys around here can't even carry on an intelligent conversation."

"Yes," Nakamura admitted, "but with a woman like that—just talking? *Eeee!* Not me. She must like you a lot, Kuwahara. It's probably all up to you. Now, don't get angry. That's just the way I look at it, that's all." He shrugged. "It's none of my business, but maybe one of these days you'll be kicking yourself. No, I don't believe in living like these irresponsible *gokudo* around this base—not with those sluts down in shacks. But you, you've got something that doesn't happen very often. Look, when a starving man is handed a dinner, he doesn't just sit and watch it—not forever." He clapped me on the arm. "You're going to kick yourself, Kuwahara!"

"Don't try to indoctrinate him," Tatsuno said. "He knows what he wants. He's found something good."

Just talking about Toyoko made me long to see her, but

there were a few days when I didn't catch a glimpse of her. Much to my disappointment, she had taken a trip to Fukuoka, "to visit some relatives." I spent those empty evenings with my friends, but wasn't a very good companion. With Toyoko away, life was more bleak than ever before. For a while the flights hadn't been so bad; after the first shock, I had become deadened, inured. But more than ever now I hated them; I felt terror again.

When she returned after less than a week, I was nearly frantic to see her. That night when she opened her door to me, I just stood staring for a moment. She had come home during the day, and hadn't been to work. As usual, she had been to the bath, and her hair, just washed again, flowed off her shoulders. "Yasuo!" She held out her hands.

"Toyoko," I replied, "I've missed you. I've been lonely. Toyoko, you'll never know how lonely I've been." She was wearing her violet *kimono,* my favorite. My hands reached out to her own, then slid up and gripped her arms. It was the first time my hands had felt a woman's arms, and they were softer, more slender, than I had imagined. They suddenly made me realize that I had grown a lot larger and stronger during the past months.

Without thinking, I pulled Toyoko to me. It was a clumsy kiss; I didn't know any better. Only for an instant did I touch her lips before she turned her head. "Yasuo!" she murmured, sounding too much like a mother. Pressing my mouth against her exquisite neck, I repeated, "Toyoko, I've missed you."

We separated and she looked at me. "I've missed you too, Yasuo." Her eyes seemed wistful.

Then I remembered. I had bought her a present—an expensive bottle of perfume, "*Kinsuru.*" I had hunted a long time for it.

"Yasuo-*chan!* How sweet! How very thoughtful and generous of you!"

Suddenly more flustered than ever, I answered, "No, it is nothing at all. It is a most miserable gift, really." Opening the bottle, she sniffed delightedly, tilting her head to the side, she dabbed some of it behind one ear, then held out her hand for me to sniff.

Later that evening, though, as we walked along a hillside above the ocean, I sensed that she was really unhappy. "Didn't you have a good time with your friends?" I inquired.

"Let's sit down," she said. "I want to talk to you." We

found a spot overlooking the water, and I waited impatiently for her to speak. Finally she said, "Yasuo, I've got something to tell you."

"What?" I demanded.

"Don't be angry with me, but I thought I ought to tell you. You see, this trip I took was to see a man, a man I've known a long time. He's an army officer." Speechless, I stared at her. Not that I hadn't suspected there had been other men. But I hadn't realized how much it would affect me, merely having her mention the existence of one. No, I had continually told myself that she was too much a sister. "He used to be stationed here. We were going to be married, but after he was transferred a few months ago—well, he changed his mind. Maybe it was just an excuse. Well, I went to see him. He wrote, asking me to. But when we saw each other again . . . Things just aren't the same any more."

"You mean you aren't going to be married?"

"No, no, it's all past now. But I wanted to tell you."

"Why?" I asked. "Why did you want to tell me?"

"I'm not sure, really. It's just that I think so much of you. I had to, that's all. You know how much you mean to me. I just wanted you to know the truth."

After that, neither of us spoke for a long time. I sat wondering, trying to decide exactly how she did feel about me. Was I nothing but a younger brother? I leaned back against the hill, hearing the sounds of night. On one side of us the ocean lounged, a great living thing. On the other, a few pricks of light marked the main part of town. Farther out lay the base—a ring of black. No bombing from the enemy yet, but they would soon be coming. How did she feel about me—really? What would she do if I reached over and pulled her to me? No, there was a wall about her. She was thinking of another man. Besides, she was like Tomika—too much.

I left her that night, feeling angry, feebly telling myself that I would not come back. But I did come back, every night that I could, even when she seemed lost in melancholy, and would hardly speak. She began to brighten after a few days, but by then I knew I couldn't go on being a brother to her forever. What Nakamura had said about her had started me thinking—no matter how much I hadn't wanted to. What Nakamura had said, and my longing during her absence. And now, knowing she'd been with another man—a man who hadn't been just a brother.

140

There were nights when we went swimming, when afterward I lay close to her on the sand, so close we touched—smelling the tang of salt. Often the nearness, the smoothness, of that warm skin made me tremble.

I didn't want that feeling; I fought it. But it was getting a firmer grip. Late one night, after one of those swims, a warm rain had fallen and, hand in hand, we had wandered back to her apartment, smelling the salt, dust, and breeze all mingled into something tantalizing.

With no light but the glow of coals in the *hibachi*, we changed into our *yukata*. Once I glanced at Toyoko, seeing the faint, red-orange glow against the bare curve of her thigh and shoulder. The rest was in shadow.

Then we went out onto the balcony, and sat listening to the bird-like wheedle of the *soba* flutes. "There are a lot of lonely women in this land tonight," Toyoko murmured.

"Are you lonely?" I asked.

"No, no, not with you, Yasuo. It's just that . . ."

"Just that what?"

"Yasuo." She placed her hand on my neck and stroked my hair. She was wearing the perfume. "It's just that . . . Oh, why couldn't you be older than you are? That's not what I mean either. Why do I have to feel about you the way I do?"

I began to tremble. "Am I such a baby to you? Before long I'll be seventeen, Toyoko. I've seen things. I've done things! I know things men—millions of older men—don't know, things they won't know, not if they live forever. Toyoko, I have to tell you . . . I can't stand it this way. It's driving me crazy. Yes, you were a sister to me at first, but not any more. Not now! I want you!"

"No, Yasuo-*chan*, please," she said.

I was stroking her face, her neck, pulling her to me, kissing her eyes, her ears, her entire face. I caught her mouth and held it fiercely against mine. For a moment she relented, her mouth moving and fluid against my own. Then as I crushed her to me, she struggled, gasping, "No, Yasuo! Please, Yasuo! You mustn't!"

But I was full of hot coals. I held her firmly, felt her breathing. "Toyoko," I cried, "I don't want to hurt you. I, I need you. We need each other! Let me prove to you I'm not a child! Let me prove it, please! I want you! I'm a man!"

"No, Yasuo, no, no. It's not right, not for either of us,

141

not now." She kept shaking her head, trying to pull free, trying to cover herself.

"Not right?" I seized her thigh. "Why? Why? Do you want me to go crazy? When will it be right? Will it be right a few days from now when I'm dead?" Her breasts were rising and falling, and I had never seen anything so exquisite. I reached out.

"No!" Toyoko gave a strangled cry, and with a violent effort pulled her leg loose, thrusting a knee in my stomach. As she began to rise I grabbed a wrist and ankle, and we tumbled into the room, wrestling, rolling over. I seized her, pinning her arms, and she stopped struggling. Now she was sobbing, violently.

Gasping, I looked into her face. She was crying like a little girl. Suddenly I felt sick. I released her wrists and pulled her *yukata* tight around her. "Toyoko, forgive me!" I pleaded. "I'm sorry, I'm sorry, I'm sorry!" I buried my face against her shoulder. Then we were both weeping.

The plaintive flute calls had subsided when we finally stretched out on our separate *futon*. From time to time I heard Toyoko sniffling, still catching her breath. Once a tide of anguish and sorrow, such as I had never experienced, inundated me. "Toyoko, please don't hate me!" I called, and I could hear my own voice fading and forlorn. She made no reply, but after a moment I heard her moving. In a little while she had dragged her *futon* in beside mine.

"I don't hate you. You know I don't hate you, Yasuo." For a while her words were hardly coherent. She lay back and felt for my hand. "Yasuo," she murmured, "I don't blame you. It—it wasn't your fault. And, please, I don't think you're a child. No, no, you aren't just a brother either. Many times I've . . . It's not that I haven't wanted you, too, Yasuo. It's just that you're so different. There's something about you— something good. Somehow . . ."

"Oh, Yasuo, I don't know what I'm trying to say. I've known something good with you—something so special. And yet . . . it could so easily be destroyed. And I would be no different then from all the rest. You know what I'm talking about, what I mean. I know you do!"

"Yes," I said, "I do," and gripped her hand. "But I have to tell you. I don't want you to think I just . . . I love you, Toyoko." I lay there listening to the clink, tinkle, clink of

142

the chimes, against the drowsy plash of waves on the shore. The rain was settling easily once more.

"I love you, Yasuo. I have since that first night." Something seemed to flow from her hand through mine, up into me. "And that first night, Yasuo, we were so lonely." Her breathing was regular now. The chimes and the sea and the rain would carry us quietly away. "So lonely," she said, "so lonely."

Part Six

23

ASHES FOR THE FAMILY SHRINE

Early in the morning I left for the base—not knowing that I would never see Toyoko Akimoto again.

The streets and lanes were quiet, and clouds were blotching part of the sky. In the fields, and between the houses, the wind swirled dust and bits of paper. It was one of those rare summer mornings, one of those strange reminders, even in the midst of heat and greenery, that winter will come again some day.

Nearing the base, I felt an empty tingling. Today I would be flying another escort mission. Okinawa. We had been briefed yesterday and would receive final instructions today. Okinawa. Who would it be this time? Another fifteen or twenty men. Lately I hadn't been checking the names. It was better that way, better, too, that I hadn't formed any close friendships at Ōita.

Already, as I flashed my pass for the gate MP, the base was beginning to vibrate. Overhead, almost out of sight, a plane cried, and I began walking fast. It was almost time for formation.

The formation over, I hurried to the mess hall, planning to eat quickly, then check over my fighter. I was more cautious in this regard than most, always making sure the mechanics had everything primed. At least I had confidence in my own flying ability now, and I was determined not to leave this world because of some trivial oversight.

Months of grueling practice were behind me—a series of dog fights, most of them hit-and-run affairs, but several good skirmishes. I was no longer the green pilot who had followed his lieutenant into battle. I had two of the enemy to my credit—verified kills. And at Ōita I had been promoted to corporal, a rank not easily attained by Japanese enlisted men.

And now, grim as the task was, I was a leader—leading

Kamikaze pilots through the enemy fighter screen, defending them to that last dive, then returning with the facts. That was my job. Who else had a more important job?

And at night? There would be Toyoko. Toyoko had said she loved me, and that was enough for the time being. I couldn't die now. Something would happen to save me. I would be invincible. A time would come when Toyoko would give me all her love, and it would be right. She would be my wife.

Today Nakamura was to fly the same mission with me. That made everything better. I had spotted him in the mess hall, ahead of me in line. My plate and bowl filled, I followed him to a table.

"*Yai, tomadachi*, pal!" I roughed his head playfully. "Seen Tatsu this morning?"

Unsmiling, Nakamura looked up. "Yes, I've seen Tatsuno."

"Well, what's the matter? Where is he?"

"Getting ready."

"Going with us? Escort now?".

"Going with us—yes. Escort—no."

Something filled my chest like a lead slab. "He's lucky," Nakamura said. "No more worries, not after noon today. You and I—we still have to wait."

As if it were a very important matter, I placed my chopsticks carefully on the table. "When did he find out? Why didn't somebody tell me before so I could have at least been with him? Why didn't you tell me?"

"It only happened day before yesterday. And you haven't been the most available man in the world this last month—you know that. You should try reading the orders sometime, Kuwahara. You don't want to miss your own name."

I locked my fingers and clamped one knuckle between my teeth, staring through the table into nothingness. "And I've hardly even seen him, lately. Since we left Hiro, I haven't even been a friend to Tatsuno! Where have I been? What have I been thinking?" Fiercely I bit my knuckle. That was the only thing that felt good just then—my teeth cutting into the knuckle.

"I tried to find you last night," Nakamura said. "I went to your girl's apartment about ten, but you weren't there."

"We were down at the beach."

"Nice! A lot nicer than being with—"

"Stop it!" I banged my fists on the table, grated my chair

145

back, and stumbled blindly out of the mess hall. Where was Tatsuno? I'd find him. I'd tell him I would die with him. I'd cover him all the way down, all the way to the ship. We'd go together. No, Tatsuno wouldn't go alone. Not my friend! I ran for nearly a quarter of a mile across the base, then stopped before I ever got to his barrack. He and his fated companions would be getting their final briefing now.

I turned and shuffled bleakly toward my own quarters. Two hours before take-off time—an hour before our last instructions. Nothing to do but wait. I wouldn't even check my Hayabusa now, not until time to go. Nakamura was waiting when I entered my billet, sitting on my cot.

Without speaking, I sat beside him. Nakamura drew a deep breath and clapped me on the leg. "I'm sorry, Yasbei," he said. "I didn't know what I was saying. I'm about ready to crack up. I really am." I gripped his arm hard.

"Don't feel bad, Yasbei," he muttered. "Tatsuno wouldn't have wanted it any different—not with you. It's just as he told me last night. We're all going the same place, and we're going soon. It's only a few days, one way or the other—no matter how you look at it. These last days . . . You've done the best thing, Yasbei. You've found somebody worth spending the time with. Something, no matter what happens."

"But not even to see him!" I choked. "Tatsuno! Do you know how long we've known each other?"

"Ever since you were about four—Tatsu told me. You couldn't have done him any good hanging around here anyway. We'd all be getting on each other's nerves. I haven't seen Tatsu much myself. He's been up in the mountains with the priest anyway."

I had to ask the next: "How's he taking it?"

"Perfectly!" Nakamura said. "Perfectly! Anyway," Nakamura continued, "I have a funny feeling about today. Today maybe we'll all get it. Today we'll all go down burning—we'll repay the emperor. I've a feeling in my bones."

Somehow the remaining time passed. It was as if there had been a blank space, then I found myself standing on the airfield, suited up, waiting to fly. There were sixteen pilots all told—four of us escorts, the remaining dozen never to return. The twelve had just grouped for final directions before an officer with a map.

We all stood at attention, respectfully listening to the commanding officer now—his parting words. A short distance away I could see Tatsuno, but he didn't look real—just a facsimile. His spirit. . . . It had already gone like the wind among the lanterns.

Around the shaved skull of each *Kamikaze* was bound a small flag, the crimson rising sun over his forehead. These departures were never conducted in a perfunctory manner. There was much ceremony, much show, toasts and valiant speeches—most of which I had already learned by rote.

Boys and girls, drafted from school to work on the base, were allowed to assemble with the squadron on these occasions. Among the fringe of onlookers a knot of girls began to weep, and then grew quiet. It was time for the commanding officer's speech.

Yes, the same words, the words I had heard so often on this runway during the past weeks—the voice droning nasally for several minutes, and then the conclusion: "And so, valiant comrades, smile as you go. . . . There is a place prepared for you in the esteemed presence of your ancestors . . . guardian warriors . . . *samurai* of the skies. . . ."

And at last it was time to sing the battle song:

"The Airman's color is the color of the cherry blossom.
Look, the cherry blossoms fall on the hills of Yoshino.
If we are born proud sons of the Yamato race,
Let us die fighting in the skies."

Then the final toast. The *sake* glasses were raised and the cry surged: *Tennoheika Banzai!* (Long live the Emperor). The *Kamikaze* were saying *sayonara* now, laughing and joking as they climbed into their obsolete planes—antiquated fighters, even trainers. The old planes didn't matter, though. It was a one-way trip. The smiles? They might remain on some of these faces to the very last. For others, those smiles began to fade as they settled into their cockpits. Maybe for a few the fear cloud would not settle until the enemy convoy loomed. And what was courage? I never knew. Who was the most courageous—the man who felt the least fear or the man who felt the most? But just then I could think of only one man.

There he was with Nakamura, walking toward me. He didn't look real. That was right; the spirit had left already. His body would mechanically fulfill the duty. What a strange smile carved on that waxen face. *Tell him! Tell him you'll cover him all the way that you'll die with him. But no, he doesn't want it, and something, something strangles all words.*

147

Your time will come soon enough, Kuwahara. Yes, by repeating those words, I could ease the sensation of guilt. I was no friend; I hadn't been for weeks. And never once had he presumed to suggest that we see each other more often.

The lead slab in my chest was heavy now, weighing me down, crushing the words. "Tatsuno . . . I . . ." Our hands met in an icy clasp. Nakamura stood by, looking down. Nakamura, a better friend than I, was giving me this final moment.

"Remember . . ." the words came, "how we always wanted to fly together?" I looked into his eyes and bowed my head.

"I will follow you soon," I whispered.

Then he gave me something. "Here," he said, "take care of this for me. It's not much to send, but take care of it."

Quickly I looked away. Tatsuno had just given me his little finger. Our doomed men always left something of themselves behind, a lock of hair, fingernails, an entire finger—for cremation. The ashes were sent home to repose in the family shrine. There, in a special alcove, the ashes would reside with the pictures of ancestors. Once yearly, a priest would enter that room to pray.

The first motors were beginning to rev, and I held onto Tatsuno as if by holding on I might preserve him. "*Sayonara,* Yasuo," he said. We fell toward each other embracing.

Without looking back, I broke away and stumbled to my Hayabusa. Not knowing how I got there, I found myself seated, fastening my safety belt, feeling the controls, adjusting my goggles. The whole base was grumbling in final preparation.

I checked the prop mixture, then pressed the starter button. One cylinder caught, a high coughing explosion, then another and another. . . . The motor blared, and shifted into a steady grumble. We were moving out—lethargic, winged beasts coming to life. Uno, a veteran with five kills, was in the lead; I was close behind him—signals coming from the control tower. Already the onlookers were in another world, withdrawn. A ring fading from the prop blasts hurled back the air, sand, bits of straw and paper.

The commanding officer, students, other pilots, the mechanics who had come to bid good-by to the ships they had nutured—all began shrinking as the strip sank beneath us.

24

THE DIVINE STORM

It was good flying weather. The seasonal rains had subsided, leaving a clear dome of blue. Within minutes, we had left the mainland behind, left the mountains, and I was thinking how Japan itself is little more than a conglomeration of mountains, great, rolling remnants of the past, when islands reared and sank like stricken monsters, when fires burst from nature's hidden furnaces. We left the shores. The shores of four islands, and the slopes that housed over seventy million people—in the crust of black-brown dwellings.

There was the re-fueling stop at Kagoshima on the island of Kyushu, about an hour after take-off. For twelve men, the last glimpse of their homeland. For twelve men, the three-hour flight to Okinawa would be their last hours on earth. Oka and Yamamoto had left three weeks ago.

A few minutes off Kagoshima we spotted a flight of B-29's escorted by Grummans, traveling toward Shikoku. Altering our course slightly, we faded into a skein of wispy cirrus clouds, and cruised on at a moderate speed. Below, the Pacific rolled, a deep, scalloped green, glinting further out under the sun, like a billion holiday sparklers.

I thought of many things during that flight to Okinawa. Home was a dream, an old wound that throbbed faintly, and not so often as it had. Toyoko? I saw her countless times, in countless ways. Sometimes just a silver face, unreal in the garden moonlight—or glowing softly beneath a lantern gateway. Sometimes the clear eyes, as they had looked at me on our first meeting. Little movements—the way she walked in her tight *kimono,* such dainty steps, one foot placed directly in front of the other.

But always there was a great void within me, and I kept hearing Nakamura's fateful augury from a few hours back in the other world; "Today we will fulfill our obligation to the emperor. I have a feeling in my bones." Nakamura, the recruit who had first befriended me during the beginning days of basic—those frightening times my loquacious friend, a practical man and a strong one.

I remembered a day long, long ago when Tatsuno and I

had run laughing through the streets of Onomichi, swatting at each other with our caps. Always the pensive one, Tatsuno, the rare friend in whom one could always confide, whose understanding went so far below the surface. "Tatsuno, Tatsuno . . ." I repeated the name, and moved on in a dream.

The waters turned back, and far ahead the clouds were merging. "One hour left," Uno's words crackled in the intercom. I glanced at him, ahead, off my right wing, and signaled acknowledgment. Uno was a squat, sinewy sergeant in his early twenties, who had known only a farmer's life and had been transformed into a cunning sky fighter. Soon, if he was lucky, he would be an ace.

Ahead, the clouds were heavier, cutting off the sparklers beneath them. Off somewhere amid that darkening water. . . .

Our *Kamikaze* were traveling in wedges of three—lethal arrows slicing toward the American ships. On and on, we cut deeper into the day. The time was close at hand and, as it drew nearer, the dry-plaster feeling in my mouth increased—something that always happened. My hands were clenching and opening—the inevitable sweating. "You're too taut, Kuwahara," I kept saying. Quick glimpses of Toyoko again. "Wait for me, Toyoko. Wait for me."

Strange how so many irrelevant thoughts kept pecking at me. They were part of my defense mechanism—sedatives against fear. Soon these last sedatives would wear off.

Long since, we had passed the small islands of Yaku and Togara, and now with Amami fading in our wake, we looked ahead. Okinawa! It was looming before us, brooding, and a throbbing in my head had started. I craned my neck, then came the jolt. Sergeant Uno waggled his wings. Far off, I saw the swaths of the first American ships. I began counting those water trails—*ichi, ni, san, shi*—twenty-five in all, and there, no bigger than seeds for the moment, in the center of that task force was our quarry, four carriers, guarded by battleships and a perimeter of destroyers.

Uno signaled again and our twelve *Kamikaze* crept ahead of us at full bore—moving into the strike at ten thousand feet. The four of us climbed slightly, following. Moments sliding by, the ships growing . . . growing . . . growing. They were beginning to open up!

At last the waiting was over. I even welcomed the fear. It would all happen fast now. Then we could return and make our reports as usual. It would be no more dangerous than ever.

Tatsuno was leading the last V in an all-but-defunct navy plane—a Mitsubishi, Type 96.

Already the twelve had opened their cockpits, and fluttered their silk scarves in the wind. Always the wind—the divine wind. Ahead and beneath them the first flak was beginning to burst in soft, black puffs, and the tracers were red lines reaching for the heavens.

Now . . . we seem to be almost on top of them! I am sweating, watching. The lead *Kamikaze* dives, dropping vertically into a barbed-wire entanglement of flak. He'll never make the carriers; that seems obvious. Instead, he's heading for a cruiser near the fringe. For a moment it looks as if he'll make it. But no—he's hit, and it's all over. His plane is a red flare fading, dropping from sight.

Everything is a blur now—a mixture of sound and color. Two more of them go the same way, exploding in mid-air. A fourth is luckier. He screams unscathed through the barrage, leveling inside the flak umbrella near the water. A hit! He's struck a destroyer right at the water line. A bellowing explosion, then another and another. It's good! It's good! The ship is in its death throes. It can't stay afloat—water plunging over the bow, stifling it. It up-ends and is gone.

Now I'm losing track of the flights. They've been scattered. The two trailing formations are forging in through the lethal blossoms. Everywhere, incredible sound and confusion. One of our planes is skimming low across the water, gunfire kicking up a thousand spouts around him. He's closing the gap, aiming straight for a carrier. Straight in—he'll score a direct hit. No, no, they got him. He's bashing into the stern, inflicting little damage.

The defense is almost impregnable. Only a gnat could penetrate that fire screen now. Two more suicides stab at the same carrier and disintegrate, splattering the water. Others have dropped like firebrands into the sea. Impossible to keep track at all now. So far I can be certain that we have sunk only one ship.

Already, only a few planes left. It's hard to discern some of them against the murky horizon. Two planes, an advanced trainer and a Mitsubishi fighter, have swerved back toward us. We circle above them, watch them complete their arcs

151

and head back in. That Mitsubishi! It's Tatsuno! Yes, I'm positive. He was in the last V—the only navy plane!

The two of them are diving, knifing for the convoy's core. Suddenly the trainer plane next to him is hit, virtually clubbed from the sky. His wing and tail rip off, and he corkscrews insanely away, out of my line of vision.

Tatsuno is alone now, still unhit, making a perfect run, better than they ever taught us in school. Tatsuno! Tatsuno! Fire spouts from his tail section, but he keeps going. The orange fingers reach out. His plane is a moving sheet of flame, but they can't stop him. Tatsuno! A tanker looms, ploughing the leaden liquid. They're closing! A hit! An enormous explosion rocks the atmosphere. For a curious instant embers seem to roll and dance. Now a staccato series of smaller bursts and one mighty blast, shaking the sea like a blanket. The tanker is going down. Gone. No trace but the widening shroud of oil.

That was my friend.

The *Kamikaze* were all gone now, so far as I could tell. We had sunk a destroyer and a tanker, wounded a cruiser and (though I didn't learn it till later) severely damaged a battleship. But I had no time to ponder our success. The Hayabusa ahead of me waggled its wings in warning. A flock of Grummans was preparing to pounce on us.

I had seen them streaking from the carrier—hornets angered at having their nests disturbed. Then I had lost track of them in the melée. Now, swiftly, two Hellcats were on my tail, three hundred yards off, firing bursts. Two more were moving up fast, maneuvering into firing position. Lead began to chew my stabilizer, and a 50-caliber slug pierced the canopy inches above my head.

Instinctively the four of us broke hard in a tight turn, Uno rolling like a leaf in the wind. The next instant we were on their tails. Uno thumped off a cannon burst, and one of the Hellcats tumbled off sidewise, sputtering, belching smoke. Near by, to my left, Nakamura's wing guns glittered. I saw this out of the corner of my eye.

Vainly I was trying to draw a bead on one of the enemy, but we were on opposite ends of a teetering balance scale. Now! I was tracking him! I sent one crushing out from the cannon and missed. Angrily I opened up with my guns, but wasn't really aiming.

Three Hellcats discernible now, and four Hayabusas. The Americans fanned in opposite directions, twisting frantically. From the corner of my eye again, I saw Nakamura opening up, saw him hit home! A Hellcat sprouted fires all along the fuselage and broke apart, chunks of it hurtling back in the slip stream. Two and two! Nakamura and I were even now. I shook my fist at him, but he didn't see me.

What a fool I was! My own foe would get away! He was bidding for altitude. I nosed after him from below, and there was his unprotected belly. I cut loose.

Realizing his predicament, the Grumman started a loop, cutting back sharply—an unwise maneuver had I not been so close. As it was, however, my bullets ate empty space behind his tail, and I looped after him, firing from a ridiculous upside-down position. Astounded, I saw pockets of smoke. A surge of proud satisfaction swept over me, but he was still game, running for the clouds.

I executed an Immelmann, righting at the top of my loop just in time to see the Hellcat explode into nothingness. Uno cut a high, crying are along the cloud fringe. He had clouted it dead center with his 25 mm cannons. Victims number six for Uno, and I felt cheated.

"Run for it!" his words came. "No more games today!" At least a dozen, perhaps two dozen, of the enemy were milling hungrily about. They had spotted me, and in every direction I could see the blue wings and white stars, the blunt snouts. My friends had vanished, and I shoved the throttle on overboost, swirling away toward the clouds.

But it was a bad move. Four or five of the enemy were roaring toward me head-on and my heart wrenched. To fight would mean swift destruction now. Instinctively I hit the stick, rolling to the left. All of them overshot, losing me. Just then, however, a lone Hellcat was dropping in a vertical spiral only a hundred yards above. A crackling sound. I'd been hit! Still, no discernible damage. I rolled once more, dropping off hard, rolling, rolling—saw sea and ships gyrating on a giant turntable, then hit a straight dive. I was dropping like a rock, knowing instinctively that several of the enemy were following.

This was my only escape now. Long hours of suicide practice would give me an advantage, and most of them would not go all the way with their faster, but less maneuverable, craft. But now, intent upon escaping the air enemy, I found myself a clay pigeon for the convoy below. Miraculously I streaked through the flak, and leveled barely above the waves. A tenacious Grumman was not so lucky! He was blasted by his own ships, hurled into the sea. A geyser was his burial marker.

Egging every molecule of strength from my Hayabusa, I roared across the water, the air around me full of death. Then I climbed, looking toward my homeland. I'd thrown most of the Americans. If I could only make the clouds . . . The outer ships were still salvoing at long range, the clouds just ahead, building into black mountains.

Just then there came a jolt, and loud clank. My plane was staggering. One lone Hellcat was closing the distance, firing like a madman from nearly six hundred yards. I'd been hit! And for a moment I was paralyzed.

I waited for the smoke, for the explosion, as the motor faltered, and began to grind—then, blessedly, caught hold. The Hellcat was closing, a ravenous shark, ripping away with his fifty-calibers. Faster, Kuwahara, faster! The clouds . . . another few seconds. . . . Then I was caught up in the mantle of a cloud. I'd make it! The enemy had tried everything in his power—everything he had on the ocean, everything he could send into the sky. The enemy had failed.

I grinned grimly into the gathering gloom. Ahead, lightning fractured the sky, and the air walls came back together with an ominous slam—something more powerful than all the ships could offer. But at least, I told myself, the elements were impersonal.

My cockpit was gradually being filled with a burning odor, and I wondered again just how much damage I'd suffered. Soon I forgot about that, though. Another problem—perhaps a much greater one. Rain was lacing my wings, coming fast. And then, a sudden deluge blotted out my vision entirely for an instant before giving way to flashing, neon spider-webs. And every crackle was followed by a stunning jar, as if truck loads of lumber were being dumped against my frail shelter.

I had flown through wind and rain before, but never had I seen such a storm as the one mounting before me. Just ahead clouds converged at all angles in a sooty maelstrom, and the rain was lashing harder. Already, water sluiced through the holes in my windshield, while the winds grew more savage. Once my motor coughed, and I held my breath, until it sounded healthy again. The burning smell had abated, perhaps because of the torrent.

My temples throbbing, I squinted through the gloom. Off somewhere lay the day, but there near the storm's gullet it was almost night. With each flash, thunder numbed the sky with reverberating concussions. Soon I was unsure of my directions, yes, completely unsure. My compass was waggling like a scales pointer under sudden pressure, and with a shock, I noted that both my gyro horizon and my turn-and-bank indicator were out of commission. No matter what awaited me out in the day, I had to leave that inferno—fast!

But which way? Angling off to the left was a sick smear of yellow. I clutched my controls and nosed toward it—a moth to light. It was increasing a little when the belly of my plane seemed to drop from under me—a down-draft. In an instant I had slipped a hundred feet, my prop clawing helplessly. It was like a blow in the stomach. The motor rattled as if at any minute it would tear loose.

Then the pressure lifted, and I was blasted upward, shaken and rolled. I emerged from that one, groggy, my head spinning. No rational means of piloting my Hayabusa now. Cut my rudder to the left, and I could just as easily be hurled off to the right. Cut my elevator upward, and I might be slammed toward the sea.

With instruments dying, the motor steadily growing more asthmatic, I was desperately tired. Only moments before, I'd grinned in the storm's face, but now my hands and arms were growing numb. I'd been flying too long. I was too tense. Even the inside of my plane revolved dizzily now, and my vision was so blurred that it would be hard to tell whether the rain ever let up or not.

All sense of time was gone. Once when the winds abated, I found myself drifting aimlessly, blinking at the blue flashes, hearing the reverberations. Like an automaton, I was flying with only one purpose—to keep going, on and on, until the great light would shine again.

Then the winds came raving back to assault me. The flashes lit a vast cloud face, its mouth breaking into a leer. My ship began to shudder and drop as though bouncing down a flight of invisible stairs. No longer were the elements impersonal. The lightning was not crackling; it was laughing. The thunder shouted, hammering with its fists. The wind, most of all, hated me—cursing, buffeting, wrenching. Was even nature with the enemy?

Suddenly a volcanic eruption of air and cloud caught beneath my wing, hurling me end over end. With no more control than a dried leaf I went spinning down a cone of blackness. Yes, this—death and oblivion!

But even in death I remembered. . . . Somewhere down the sky's long hallway, something willed the battered, shuddering metal back, exerted effort against strange controls.

I was flying level, the leaden waves curling at my belly, scudding with froth. As from a distance, sounds of the motor rose and fell, and my ship seemed to jump along. It seemed I was back with my first glider, being towed across the turf at Onomichi High School.

Even lower I settled. Low, so low! Just a dipping of one wing, just a few degrees, and the ocean would have me once and for all. Why fight it? It always got what it wanted. Only a matter of moments, a matter of degrees. . . . But there was still a perverse spark within me. No, I wasn't afraid. I would taunt the ocean, dipping my wings never quite far enough—tantalizing the waves. They knew how to hypnotize, so well, and they would take me soon. But not until I had laughed—as the lightning had laughed at me.

Suddenly the water flashed green. An instant later it had turned white-hot, blinding me. I kept blinking, till the pain eased. I was in a world of burnished gold.

Nothing now but water and sky. I climbed to a thousand feet, and droned ahead, soaking up light. It took a while for the awareness to come. I was alone—the only man in this strange, beautiful world—lost amid the lonely reaches of sun and sea.

The motor sputtered, and I glanced at my fuel gauge: only twenty-five gallons—little time left. Apprehensively, fearing the American ears that would now be listening beyond the horizon, I began to signal. No answer. I waited and tried again. Still, no reply. My fighter kept winging ahead, staunch once more—wonderful creature! But now, after everything else to run out of fuel—to expire slowly, like a strong man with his wrists cut. It seemed hopeless—but there was the faintest . . . I cut the air-control valve to its thinnest mixture, cut the propeller cycles down—below 1,800 rpm's. Much less, and I'd be in for a stall.

I signaled again, caught my breath and waited. An answer!

China! "This is Nanking. . . ." The message was coming! I had made connections.

A few degrees left, and straight ahead was Formosa. In less than twenty minutes I would be there. Soon. . . . Yes, I could see it, seeming to rise and fall like a great ship. The motor purred, steady, true.

Once I looked back. I had a feeling that I shouldn't, but I looked back. Somewhere off in the golden afternoon was Okinawa. Somewhere lurked the enemy task force—only twenty-three ships now, instead of twenty-five. Somewhere, drifting in the sea, were the remains of Tatsuno, and the others. No pain any more—not for Tatsuno.

And there—hanging slumbrous now, far behind—was the storm. "The divine storm" had saved me, as it had saved my people centuries before.

25

THE LONELY PLACE

My wounded craft made the remaining distance to Formosa and I landed at Taihoku, the main base. Without even resting, I was immediately sent to a smaller base, near by, not far from Kiirun. There I was to remain for nearly two weeks, because of insufficient fuel. Yes, conditions by now were that desperate. The bases in Formosa were eating their final rations. Barely enough fuel for the suicides, who left each day.

Despite my exhaustion, my first concern upon landing was my Hayabusa. During the months, and now especially, I had developed an affection for that ship. To me, my Hayabusa had become a living creature, a creature I understood, even loved. Somehow along the way it had acquired a soul. Yes, it had helped me vanquish enemies and, even when I had been utterly helpless, my Hayabusa had bored on through the storm.

Parts of the tail assembly and the tip of my right wing had been sheared off. There were several bullet holes—four of them running through the fuselage—gaps from two to three inches in diameter. The motor had stopped lead, but, amazingly enough, had never quite conked out.

And finally, I examined two holes through my canopy. One slug had gashed the dome, and another had pierced the glass not four inches above my head. My life had teetered on a razor edge.

No irreparable damage in any event. Beneath the shade of some banana trees, fringing the strip, I rested beside my plane before making my routine report.

Two mechanics were approaching in the distance, and all about me preparations were under way for tomorrow's suicide attack. Apparently the airfield had been bombed a short time before my arrival, for crews were filling in the craters, tamping the dirt down. Dead tired, I eased back against a tree trunk, waiting for the mechanics. I wondered what it would be like to repair planes instead of flying them. The mechanics felt a great devotion to their planes, also.

Then I began thinking of Toyoko—wondering how soon I would see her once more. And the air alarm shrilled! Without the slightest additional warning, twenty-five Grummans, in waves of five, came growling off the jungle roof. Immediately the two mechanics turned tail, and the construction crew scattered across the concrete rectangle in every direction! Too late! The first flight was roaring in on them. I remained where I was, hearing the tattoo of guns, watching bullets spatter the cement.

One man reached the jungle, plunging headlong into it. But the two mechanics were trapped in the lead hail. The slower one tumbled as though struck by an invisible truck, while his companion, just short of cover, turned a flip-flop, rolling over and over.

Four men from the construction crews had escaped the first wave, and were feigning death in the middle of the field. But it was a poor ruse. As the second wave riddled them, one figure half-rose and fell back convulsing.

The enemy fighters cavorted about, blasting everything in sight, having a marvelous time. Not the slightest interference. A hanger began to flame, a line of obsolete *Kamikaze* planes was devasting, and several of the remaining fighters were knocked out.

Finally, their ammunition spent, the Grummans vanished into the sunset. The trees and their shadows had afforded camouflage for me and my Hayabusa. Wearily I got to my feet, and crossed the field, fading into a smoke screen. There amid the haze were the corpses, grotesquely sprawled

—a leg bent beneath a body, a head swiveled freakishly, a severed arm, entrails splattered. A foot short of cover lay one of the mechanics, half his head gone. Drafted schoolboys—all of them.

Detached, I began to search for the orderly room. Tomorrow there would be more attacks. More men would probably die. More aircraft would be destroyed. But now I wanted only one thing—to report in and be assigned a bed.

Half an hour later I collapsed on a cot. Not far from me three men were playing cards at a table, laughing, and the room was heavy with cigarette smoke. When had I last seen Toyoko? It seemed weeks ago. It couldn't possibly have been only fourteen or fifteen hours before. Tatsuno. . . . He had gone ages ago. Oita was a dream base, far far away from this tropical isle. Where was Nakamura now? And the other two escorts Uno and Kimura? I sank into a delirious sleep, knowing that I would relive all that had happened, over and over again during the night. I remember coming to the surface of consciousness once—stifling, damp heat—and a voice saying, "Take it easy, fighter pilot. Just relax."

For two weeks I remained at that remote base as an instructor. It was a unique task—teaching men the best way to die. Daily, the fated groups left. One after another, I saw them go, always circling the field once, always waggling their wings in a last *sayonara*.

Then after their departure, signal men at the base would listen for the high, long-drawn beep—an inevitable signal from the flight leader that the enemy was in sight, that the attack had begun. Moments later, like scissors cutting a taut cord, the sound would end. *Sayonara,* you loyal sons of Japan!

It wasn't until the day after my arrival at Formosa that I learned what had become of the other escorts. Uno was the only one who had returned to Oita. Nakamura and Kimura had not been heard of, and I had also been reported missing. Uno had seen me plunging toward the convoy with the Hellcats close behind, and had given up all hope for my survival. There was a possibility that the other two might have escaped to some island along the Ryukyu chain extending southwest below Kyushu. But it was doubtful. No word.

And now, with several days gone, there was no hope for either of them. Something told me that Nakamura had joined Tatsuno in the ocean. Nakamura. The last time I had seen him he was gunning down an enemy. He had gone like a true *samurai*. He had known it was coming. My sorrow? It was a different kind, that wouldn't really blossom until later.

All my closest friends were gone now, and I waited alone in the sultry afternoons of Formosa each day after the *Kamikaze* had departed. Death hovered in the air those slow days—and I had nothing to do most of the time but think. Occasionally I wandered to some empty beach, sometimes to swim, but most of the time just to sit on the shore, letting the tide fizz around my bare toes, thinking—all my thoughts in the past, mostly of Toyoko. There were times when I cried out for her. Undoubtedly, she thought I was dead now. It was impossible to imagine that we had known each other only a few short weeks. I could never keep track of time any more. The last attack at Okinawa could have happened months before.

Only one day prior to my departure from that lost island, something happened which helped to sap our waning morale. Eight suicides had racketed into the sky, circled, dipped their wings, then headed out. As I watched, one of them turned back. For a moment I thought he was having engine trouble. Then as he neared the field, someone cried, "He'll never land! Coming in too high! Too fast!"

"He's heading for the hangar!" another yelled. "Do something! Fire engines!" I hit the dirt just as a blast quaked the area. He had plunged into the main hangar, and the flames were climbing. Within seconds the hangar was a holocaust. Sirens wailed. Men scurried, shouting, swearing. Somehow, the fire trucks and the men seemed ridiculous.

I despised their fumbling attempts and watched calmly. When at length the hoses were going, there was a tremendous explosion within the hangar, then another. Again and again—it kept blasting forth.

Each time, the firemen staggered back, stumbling and falling, releasing the hoses, which thrashed about like pythons. Twenty of the best remaining fighters were exploding like popcorn—a beautiful fireworks display. Thousands of gallons of stored fuel went next. Nothing could be salvaged.

Later, a letter was discovered among the dead man's possessions. Apparently written that morning, it contained some terse statements regarding Japan's plight and the futility of war, and the conclusion read: "My fellow comrades, by the time you read these words I will be dead. Do not judge me in anger. What is done, is done for a good reason. Perhaps our leaders, and men everywhere, will come to realize the stupidity of war some day, and perhaps through my own feeble and miserable efforts some of you may live. Japan's surrender is imminent, and by the time you read these words there will be twenty fewer planes for men to waste their lives in." Two of his friends tore up that letter and devoured it, but its message was soon rumored about the base.

Luckily, my Hayabusa had been repaired and fueled before the destruction of the gasoline. The following morning I winged off over the jungle, leaving that wretched, lonely place forever.

26

LIGHTER THAN A FEATHER

It was the last of June, 1945, when I landed again at Oita. I had flown back through China, crossing over the East China Sea to avoid American fighters.

Frantic to see Toyoko, I rushed to the orderly room to report in. How would she react upon seeing me this time? Had anyone told her I was still alive? I hadn't known anyone well enough to ask the favor. No one even to get in touch with, anyway—only official communications. Personal letters hadn't left Formosa for a long time.

"You're to report to the commander of your squadron immediately, Corporal Kuwahara."

I stared at the desk sergeant. "Immediately?"

"Yes, immediately!"

"You mean I can't even . . .?" I turned and shuffled out the door. My eagerness turned to a sharp uneasiness. Nothing to do but clean up and change as quickly as possible.

In the barracks a thousand thoughts ran through my mind. I had supposed that Uno's report two weeks ago was sufficient. What more could I tell Captain Tsubaki than Uno had told him? Soon I was striding across the base. What could he want? Couldn't the captain even give me time to catch my breath? Didn't he have any idea that I had just flown all the way from Formosa?

As is sometimes customary with officers, Captain Tsubaki

failed to acknowledge me for a moment after I had entered his office. I reported, and held the salute.

The captain glanced up, fanned his eyebrow, and went back to his papers. "Be seated, Kuwahara." He waited for a moment, then looked at me—the same searching expression I had seen months before—on New Year's Day. "How are conditions in Formosa?" he asked.

At first I was tongue-tied, not knowing what he expected. "You mean, honorable captain . . ."

"Planes, ammunition, fuel, morale! You know."

I fought an urge to be evasive, then said frankly, "There is little left—of any of those things. The enemy grows stronger every hour, honorable captain—everywhere! Why deny it?" I knew Tsubaki well enough by this time. I could talk to him. Anyway, I was in no mood for self-restraint. The utter futility of that base near Kiirun had added to my bitterness. Yes, I agreed with that mother in the Hiroshima hospital, with Tatsuno, with the man who had destroyed the hangar at Formosa—with millions of others! No matter how I loved my country, we were dying senselessly.

"All right, Kuwahara," he said, "let's have your report for 10 June. I will verify it against Uno's." I reported the action as I had recorded it, and was unable to account for two of the suicides. At this, Tsubaki pounded his desk, exclaiming, "Incompetence! We didn't send you out on a picnic, Kuwahara!"

His rebuke didn't ruffle me much, because it was almost obligatory, and he seemed to be agitated over bigger things, really. Tsubaki gave a sigh. "You lost your best friend on that mission, didn't you?"

I looked straight at him, then down at the floor: "Two of my best friends, captain."

The captain hadn't really been interested in my report; he had to know something else. "Kuwahara, what were you thinking . . . when you saw your friends go? How does it make you feel?"

"I wanted to die with them."

Our eyes met. "Really, Kuwahara? Is that really what you felt? Didn't you still want to keep living—no matter what?"

"Well, I—"

"Did you hate the Americans? Was there a burning hatred in your heart? Did you want to destroy them all?"

"Sometimes I hate the Americans, Captain. Sometimes . . ."

"Yes?"

"Sometimes I hate—"

Tsubaki finished my sentence: "The stupid leaders . . . in Tokyo?"

I took a long breath, and felt myself quiver slightly. "Yes! I hate them for what they have done to this nation, for their eternal lies to our people! The *Daihonei*. . . . Even after the bombs have fallen on their heads, their damned voices say all is well. 'All is well, people of Japan! Fear not, gullible, stupid people of Japan! This is all part of the plan!' Whose plan?" I buried my face in my hands, amazed at myself even as I choked down the sobs.

When I looked up, the captain was staring out the window. For a full minute he looked toward the ocean. Once he cleared his throat and swallowed. He spoke quietly. "Boys—fifteen, sixteen, seventeen-year-old boys—out there over Okinawa . . . all that fire coming up." The captain's eyes were hollow, and his face had grown thinner since we'd left Hiro. "And I, I have to send them." How Tsubaki had changed!

"Corporal Kuwahara?" He kept looking out the window.

"Yes, captain."

"You have a fine record. Seen a lot of war, this last year, haven't you? A lot of sorrow, a lot of death. You've experienced more than a million other men will, in a million years. Of course you could have been sent long ago, but you have been of great value to your country." We looked into each other. "I would change it, if I could, Corporal Kuwahara. Believe me, I would change the whole world. But I am only the commander of a doomed squadron. You see, Kuwahara, even Uno, every man that can fly must. . . . All of them, soon!"

Yes, my hands were shaking. So were the muscles in my arms and legs. There was nothing I could do about that. I closed my eyes, just closed them and waited until the words came—as if a priest were sitting before me: "Are you prepared?"

As if listening to a record of my own voice, I heard the words: "Yes, honorable captain. I am honored to be deemed worthy. I wish to go as soon as possible."

How long have I waited for this? At last, at last it had come. It had really come. Strange relief now, emptiness. My veins were filled with air. If I didn't keep hold of the chair,

I would float. Somehow the dead weight was gone. If I could just get up and go right now, without thinking about it, before anything changed . . .

"You will return to Hiro as soon as you have recuperated a little, and had your meal. You will receive final orders at Hiro."

"Hiro?"

"Yes, some of it has been restored."

"But Captain Tsubaki, why so soon? I just landed."

Too many questions had made him crisp again. "Because those are the orders, Kuwahara. They're in bad need of base protection. Hardly a fighter around the place. We expect to get a good part of the Fourth back there eventually—what's left of it."

One final query: "How soon. . . . When will my missions be, captain?"

Obviously, Tsubaki wanted to have done with me now. All the military brusqueness returned. I was once more his inferior. "A week, maybe two, maybe more. I can't say."

I stood and saluted. "Thank you, captain. *Sayonara.*"

"*Sayonara,* Corporal Kuwahara."

I left, and headed for my quarters, to pack my few belongings. The air force would never let a man stay in one place very long; there was never a place he could call a home, really, not even a barracks he could call his own—they were always juggling men around. I passed the quarters where Nakamura had stayed, looked further on to where Tatsuno had been. Their belongings would have been returned to their homes by now. I still had that finger in my plane. I would sent it to Tatsuno's family when I got back to Hiro.

Thoughts of Toyoko began pounding at me, and my eyes blurred. Then I clenched my teeth. All this stupid bawling! Nothing would ever make me bawl again. Nothing! *So you won't see her. So what? So she's got another man now. What does it matter? Who are you, Kuwahara? You're nobody! You're expendable, remember. You are living in a vacuum, Kuwahara.*

"Be resolved that honor is heavier than the mountains, while death is lighter than a feather." Without any logical process of association those words came to me as I left the barracks. "Death is lighter than a feather." That last part I held on to, repeating, chanting it over and over in my mind. Perhaps I could produce a self-hypnosis.

Just before leaving Oita I encountered a bomber pilot with whom I had formed a casual acquaintanceship. "*Yai*," I hailed him. "You still go to the Tokiwaya?"

"*Un*," he nodded, "Why?"

"Do you remember my girl, Toyoko—Toyoko Akimoto?"

"*Un*," he grinned, "the nice one—long hair and . . ." He made motions with his hands, then smacked his lips against his thumb and finger tips.

"Well, she thinks I'm . . ." I felt foolish all at once. "She doesn't know that I ever came back from Okinawa. I'm leav-for Hiro and . . ."

His smile faded. "All right, Kuwahara, I'll tell her."

As we walked away from each other, I stopped. "Hey, Takahashi! Maybe you'd better not tell her anything. Forget everything I said, will you? Just forget it!"

Takahashi nodded, and gave me a combination salute-wave. "Okeh, Yasbei!"

Ha! He called me 'Yasbei.' He was a good man. I wished that I had known him better.

As I walked toward my fighter an odd thing happened. I spied a tiny gray feather in some weeds near the strip. As if it might escape, I picked it up cautiously—peered at it. Then I held it out and let it fall. Such an easy, drifting descent. I stared at it, saw it tumble along the concrete. I turned to go, then stopped once more. Crazy! Oh, how crazy you are, Yasbei.

I picked the feather up and put it in my pocket.

27

BATTLE WITH THE GIANTS

Hiro again! I'd been away less than two months. I might as well have been gone for a year. What was time? My seventeen months in the Imperial Army Air Force had been almost as long as all the rest of my life in Onomichi.

Hiro! So odd to be back once more, not fifty miles from my home. The base was different now, of course, much of it still complete ruin. Never had I expected to feel nostalgia for Hiro. But now I felt it—for the old Hiro I'd known as a trainee.

I walked past my basic-training barracks, and wondered if The Pig was still around to instill men with "the spirit." No men in that barracks. Those next to it had been burned out—not much going on about the base now. I entered, and wandered through the long, empty rooms. Time was relative, even to the dust. Dust lay deep, the dust of centuries—on the lockers, along the empty bed frames. Few things are more lonely than a moribund military installation, than walking through barracks making footprints in the dust. The hollow lockers vibrate if you tread too heavily—a desolate sound. Empty bedsprings are worse than skeletons.

In a corner were two ball bats. Hefting one, I blew on it, felt its smoothness: *"Yamatodamashii Seishinbo,"* a ball bat, for instilling the fighting spirit. What an amazing invention. I looked at the bed that had been mine, then at the one that had been Nakamura's. It still didn't seem true that he had gone.

Nothing to do but wait now, wait while the days expired. There were a few fighters at Hiro—a few pilots filtering back daily—all returning to wait. We were alerted, restricted to the base, and the time languished about us, stifled us in its vapor.

Only an occasional air battle provided any interruption. We fought with abandon, not caring much whether we were shot down or not. And, strangely enough, our very daring seemed to preserve us. Two of us downed an enemy Mustang P-51 in a surprise attack above Kure one day, then fled before the Americans even knew what had happened. As our victim plummeted into the bay, I decided that there was only one answer as far as air battles were concerned: Don't be afraid. It gave you special magic. Attack the enemy before he attacks you. Then disappear. Now that there was no hope, it was easy to attack fearlessly. I knew how to use the clouds and the sun. The enemy could send a million planes—no matter. We would always be there, a few of us, ready to slash at their tails—send a few more on their way to hell.

A week passed—two weeks—nearly a month. Incredible! I was still waiting, and nothing had come down by word of mouth, or in writing. Why were they waiting?

July was fading when we learned that a force of B-29's was flying southwest of Osaka. It seemed probable that they would pummel Osaka, then split, striking Matuse and Okayama. An indication that Japan was breathing her last, only four of us were picked to lock with them over Okayama, about thirty minutes flight from our base. Four of us, a lieutenant, a sergeant, another corporal and I, covenanted together shortly before our departure. Today we would send one of those thunderous Superforts to its death.

Having calculated the exact time of contact with the 29's, I did some additional planning. Our flight would carry us over Onomichi. Why not stage a brief aerobatic performance for the students at Onomichi High School—perhaps even for my own family and neighbors? Why not? I spoke to my three companions. They were enthusiastic.

Only a short while before take-off I sat down to write a message, just a few words of devotion to my family. I didn't know what to say. Should I tell them? No, no sense in it. None at all. They would find out soon enough. But I had to get a message to them. It was apparent from their own communications that my letters weren't getting through, and I had received little mail from them for a long time.

After pondering a while, I merely told them that I was well, that I hoped they were. I almost wondered whether my family still existed. More and more they were becoming unreal to me, and there were disquieting moments when I could no longer envision their faces.

I placed the message in a metal tube, and attached a white streamer. My last words to my family had to be delivered personally.

Not long after the take-off, I was looking down on familiar territory—the shipyards, the shore line where the fishermen dwelt, some of the main buildings of town. Many of them had been demolished. The radio station was still standing. And there, further on, was the school, a little further, my home neighborhood—the whole city lying among the Senkoji Mountains.

A group of students on the athletic field gazed up as we began to drop. I plummeted down, buzzing the school, my companions close behind. As we powered into a vertical climb I glanced back and was astonished to see the students scattering for cover.

Shaking my head, I chuckled. Green kids!

The lieutenant's voice crackled over the intercom. "Don't even know their own planes!"

"Maybe they haven't seen any before!" I fired back, then stopped laughing. Maybe they *hadn't* seen any—for a long time. A moment later, however, they emerged and began waving. With only a few seconds to spare, we plunged at them, spiraling crazily, pulling out at treetop level, rocking the buildings. We made our third pass, arching over the field, banking hard to avoid the close-circling mountains. Students had flooded from every exit by now, and were waving wildly. I could see their faces clearly, practically hear their cries.

Moments later, we circled over my own home, but saw no one familiar. Cutting low, I sent the message fluttering earthward. People were emerging from their houses. Someone would see it and deliver it to my family. It was a peculiar sensation. My home was easy enough to spot, but it looked different from the air. Everything was different from the air, and I had not returned to Onomichi, not really.

As the city fell behind, I began wondering what would become of it once we were conquered. Would the Americans show any decency? Would they be humane, or would they treat my people like cattle? A vanquished nation is spared no humiliation, I thought. A vanquished nation is plundered and used. The upturned faces and fluttering hands of those schoolgirls. . . . What would become of those young girls? How many would the enemy use?

How many of those people were still being duped? How many still harbored hope? Those people, some of them, still thought that *Kamikaze* pilots always died gloriously, believing that, for each of our men destroyed, an enemy ship was sunk. It was frustrating. Something turned inside me, and I began to swear. Today the enemy would pay. Today I would let the enemy feel my anger.

My thoughts were soon cut off. We were approaching Okayama and, according to schedule, the B-29's were moving in—only six of them heading eastward at about fifteen thousand feet, flanked by a dozen Grummans. The 29's were stupendous giants—nothing like the 17's our pilots had tangled with earlier in the war. Six of them—lethal leviathans trailing vapor against a purple sky.

The lieutenant signaled, and I clamped my lips as we hove around to begin the climb. The enemy was not yet aware of us. The Japanese Air Force, once so deadly, was now only a mockery. They probably weren't even looking for us—

just lumbering stolidly on their way. Relentless! Unfeeling! The Americans just kept coming, more and more, bigger and bigger.

Not until we had tumbled from the sun were they aware of us. Lining the rear Fortress in my range finder, I opened up the guns. The 29's answered with a vicious barrage, and the Grummans swarmed into action.

I moaned down after the lieutenant in a vertical slice and, just before completing my pass, saw his plane shudder. An instant later, he ploughed straight into our target. I rolled off instinctively, taking the shock across my belly, roaring away from a yellow-orange burst. Scarcely realizing what had happened, I lammed the stick back and jerked out of the dive at over five G's, wavering, nearly tearing my wings off. For several seconds the blood left my head, and when I came out of it, the remaining bombers had fanned and were swerving to avoid the same fate as their teammate.

So suddenly! Both the lieutenant and the B-29—gone. Incredulous, I climbed toward the sun, arched back and gave chase. The huge planes were extraordinarily fast, and it took some time for me to close the gap. As I moved in after the trailing bomber, he was weaving like a shuttle, and the Hellcats were eating up the sky with little coordination.

Ah, this would be the run of runs! I wasn't afraid! Stick over left. Over I angled, balancing on my wing tip—then came charging at him, twisting on the axis, aileron rolling down at over five hundred miles an hour. Each time that silver hulk flashed in my sights I opened up. He was looming big, moving very fast—waist, turret, and tail guns all blaring away at me in a withering barrage, graphing the whole sky with red lines.

But I was flying as I had never flown. As I closed in, the mammoth curved off from the rest of the flight, apparently expecting to be rammed. My tracers arched, seeming to curve, drawing a seam along his wing and fuselage. I'd made contact! The giant was coughing smoke! It was then that a mighty surge of elation swept through me—like strong hands lifting me up.

I never did see the 29's death, however. She was losing altitude, but still game. As I screamed past her massive rudder, intent on the kill, the tail guns ripped at me, and lead clattered, ravaging my fuselage. I opened into a wild, twisting barrel roll.

But now the Grummans had picked me up. Four of them buzzed down, lobbing with their cannons, shooting poorly. Pulling out, I cleaved off to the right, then hit the stick and rudder pedal, snapped over to the left, resumed speed, and flared, grabbing for the sun.

The evasive action, perfectly executed, threw all of them but one. Trailing the others, he'd anticipated me. I circled, pressing for altitude. Completing a full 360 degrees, I glanced over my shoulder. The Hellcat slightly above was trying to cut inside my circle, banking so close that I could distinctly see the pilot, the sun glinting on his goggles, his white teeth flashing in a determined grin. A confident American. I'll never forget that look, because suddenly I was afraid, my veins filling with water—not afraid for myself as much as for another reason. Somehow that expression symbolized so completely the hopelessness of our situation—something Japan could cope with no longer.

In no mood for a contest, I rolled over into a vertical spiral —straight down in a fifteen thousand foot plunge. Two fighters, trying to sneak up under my belly, fanned off, startled, as I bored down at them, missing the closest one by less than fifty feet. To hell with him!

Down, down, down, spinning, spinning—at last dropping straight. Pulling out perilously near the ocean, I gunned homeward at full throttle. Despite my morbid feelings of a minute before, I rejoiced momentarily in our good fortune. In addition to the '29 destroyed by our suicide, another had been mortally wounded. How I wanted to claim that giant for my own! How I wanted to verify that kill, to see her hit the water!

Later, I learned that a '29 had gone down, not far from Okayama, its crew bailing out over the inland sea.

Part Seven

28

HIROSHIMA

It was August 1, 1945. I had returned from a reconnaissance flight near Matsue to learn that someone had paid me a visit. "Your sister was here to see you," the desk sergeant said. "I'm sorry we couldn't allow her to stay, but you know we can't have any civilians on the base now." I nodded. "She left you these," he said.

Thanking him, I left for my barracks carrying an envelope, and a tiny parcel. Sitting on my cot, I opened the note: "Yasuo-*chan*, we received your message, and were overjoyed to hear from you—the first word in many long months. We didn't know what had become of you. But now, to know that you are back near us once more—just having you near —makes us feel better, even though we cannot see you.

"How proud of you we are, Yasuo-*chan!* We know that you are bringing great honor to the emperor, your country, your family. I love you for this, my brother, for your courage—but, always, more for what you have been to me, what we have been to each other. I speak now not only for myself but for your father, your mother, and your brothers as well. Wherever you may go, whatever you may be doing, our love goes with you. Each day I pray for you at the shrine, and in my heart—many, many times—to the Father of all men. Your sister, Tomika."

Over and over again I read those words, and a great longing swept over me, like a tide. If I could only have seen her— just looked at Tomika once more. The tide ebbed. "No! It's better this way!" After a while, I opened the little parcel. For a long time I sat bowed, staring at her gift, feeling the softness against my palm. Then my fingers closed over it. Tomika had sent me a lock of her hair.

A torpid August 1 merged with an August 2. Over a month since my meeting with Captain Tsubaki. Incredible! Why didn't the word come? Why? What were they waiting for?

The night of August 3, I tossed feverishly. Death was no longer my greatest fear. Waiting was my greatest fear. No hope now. Benighted though my country was, I estimated that her surrender would still not take place for many months. If the final word would only come. If it didn't come soon, very soon, I might take the easy way out—a sharp knife, a painless little cut across the wrists. 'There is nothing honorable in dying for a lost cause. There is nothing honorable. . .' The words were ringing clear once more, just as they had that day in the hospital. No, I would wait no longer, suffer no more for a lost cause. I would die the easy way—to escape the hard way. But no, no—still I would be dishonoring my family if I took the easy way. No matter how I felt about a lost cause, I couldn't humiliate them. *Wait, Kuwahara. Sit and wait. Grit your teeth. Clench your fists. Swear. Pray to God. Curse him if you have to. But wait. Don't let me bring dishonor! Don't let me bring dishonor! Keep me in the skies, striking at the enemy . . . until the word comes! Yes, fighting is the best thing now—the only thing.*

August 4. I found myself praying many times that day. That night I tore at my hair. I knew where a sharp knife was. *God, send me an enemy plane. Don't make me wait here! Don't make me wait!*

At four in the morning, August 5, I sat up suddenly, wiped the sweat from my body, and began to pace the floor. I was seeing things in a different perspective. What did it matter how I died, just so I got it over with? I didn't have a family! Just a dream.

It was cooler outside. I walked around and around the barrack in my bare feet. Gray everywhere, leaden. In just a minute I would go get the knife. I would kneel there by the side of the barracks—dark and cool. No, I was being ridiculous. No, not after this long. For a moment I cursed the entire world. Nothing would make me go out like a coward. *Now . . . go in and lie down. Go to sleep before the feeling changes again. You'll make it, Kuwahara . . . somehow. Think about something. . . . Toyoko. No, better not. Toyoko makes you think of that last night together. Then think of Tatsuno—Nakamura too. You weren't a real friend. Yes, guilt, a bad taste—that only one thing can dispel. Think of someone else. Toyoko! No, not Toyoko, no! No! Think of your sister, your mother. Ah, you can see their faces plainly for some reason—even hear their voices again.*

172

An hour before reveille, I sank into a feverish semi-consciousness.

And that day . . . I received written orders. On August 8, I would take off for the last time. At last, at last I really knew—there was something definite. The time had come and now it seemed almost an anticlimax. I actually wanted it to be worse! Peace would come in only three days. Yes, I could live another three days.

The next morning I would be granted a two-day pass. A two-day pass! Such was the Japanese Military's magnanimity to its fated sons. But I had already decided not to use that pass—thinking that it would be better never to see family or friends again. I had thought about it long. I had banished the idea from my mind.

Then, early on the morning of August 6, I burst into the orderly room. "My pass! Do you have a two-day pass here for me?"

"Ummm, let's see: Kimura . . . *Ha!* Kuwahara! But you were supposed to have filled out the book last night, corporal. . . . Well, go ahead, sign—hurry. Date it August 5, or it will be my neck. No, damn it! Not on that page! Over here."

"Thank you, sergeant." With trembling hands I scrawled my signature, destination, time of departure, time of return. Moments later I had hooked a ride in an army truck headed for Hiroshima. It wouldn't take long to get home from there. I was returning . . . to be with the people I loved. I should have known that the pull of home would be too great. How foolish I had been.

There was a sudden enchantment about the land, a beauty I had almost forgotten. The truck jolted and clattered over the pocked road, nearly jarring my teeth loose at times, but I didn't mind. I was looking at the green rice, the narrow canals, and the darkening mountains. I had almost forgotten the magic of early mornings. Suddenly I was very happy. Suddenly I felt that for two days I could place myself on a peaceful island, a final one, but a good one. Two golden days. Perhaps when they ended I could accept death. Perhaps death, as the poets had said, would be sweet. It would really be lighter than a feather. I still had that little feather with me, for some reason.

Maybe God—if there was a God—would make it easy for me from now. "Make it easy for me! Make it easy for me!" Those words drummed in my mind, and I pressed my hands hard against my head, feeling the force of every rock and depression in the road.

Yes, it was working. God was really hearing me. I kept repeating the words, and my soul began to relax as though a breeze were sweeping through. Two golden days. Nothing beyond that. Nothing mattered. That was everything, and there was absolutely nothing else to worry about.

I left the truck on the outskirts of Hiroshima at about 7:30 A. M., and a few minutes later boarded a streetcar. Before leaving the city for Onomichi, I intended to visit a friend at the Second General Army Headquarters. Leaving the streetcar, I heard it rumble off along the tracks, emitting a lonely tootle in the distance. Then I began walking along Shiratori Street toward the headquarters. The sky was slightly overcast, and even at that early hour it was growing sultry.

Already small bands of children were skittering about the streets, blessedly unaware that the world was changing, that they would ever have to become men and women. There were haunted ruins for them to venture within, strange places just for them, ashes for them to shuffle through in their bare feet.

"Ohayo gozaimasu," a business man greeted me. I returned his good morning and continued along the street. Grocers and magazine vendors had already opened the shutters on their flimsy huts. Once I stopped to buy an orange.

Further on a wrinkled woman stopped me: "Please tell me the truth," she rasped. "Why is it that I no longer see Japanese planes in the sky?" I looked into that face, withered like a dried apple, at the ash-silver strands of hair. The eyes were still alert. "Tell me the truth, young man." She hunched, blinking, stoic, waiting for the whip, wanting it.

Gently I laid my hand on her shoulder, and looked at the pavement. I wished that I could go somewhere with that ancient obaa-san and just sit with her for a while. "Old mother, there are few planes left. Before long it will be all over —and we won't have to hide from the bombs any more." Her claw closed on my hand, almost hurting it, and we parted.

Moments later, I heard the air raid sirens—a small concern to me, since two planes had already passed over while I was on the streetcar. The lone '29 above scarcely seemed worth considering at first. If I were only up there now in my Hayabusa, I'd rise with the sun, under his belly, and begin pumping them out from the cannons. But there wasn't a Japanese plane anywhere. The '29 could meander at will like a grazing animal.

I kept watching him from time to time, however. There was something a little too placid about that droning. So slow, so smug. Something . . .

When I was less than half a mile from the General Headquarters, a tiny speck separated from the silver belly above, and the plane moved off, picking up speed. No bigger than a marble, the speck increased to the size of a baseball. A parachute. Speculations were being made:

"What are they up to now?"

"More pamphlets?"

"Yes, more propaganda—more of the same old thing."

All their mutterings were cut off. Suddenly a monstrous, multi-colored flash bulb went off directly in my face. Concentrated heat lightning stifled me. A blinding flicker—blue, white and yellow. So fast it might not have really happened at all. Something inside my own head, perhaps. I sensed this last more than thought it.

I threw up my hands against the fierce flood of heat. A mighty blast furnace had opened on the world.

Then came a cataclysm which no man will ever completely describe. It was neither a roar, a boom, nor a blast. It was a combination of those things with something else added— the fantastic power of earthquakes, avalanches, winds and floods. For a moment nature had focused her wrath on the land, and the crust of the earth shuddered.

I was slammed to the earth. Darkness, pressure, choking and the clutches of pain . . . a relief as though my body were drifting upward. Then nothing.

Minutes, hours, even days—it was impossible to tell how long I remained unconscious. A rumbling noise overhead, perhaps a cart, seemed to awaken me. No thoughts at all at first, just a vague sensation of being alive. As my senses slowly returned, a personality began to form. Eventually it came to me. I was Corporal Yasuo Kuwahara, and I was buried alive, under a mass of debris.

My legs were pinned down but I worked an arm free enough to clear some of the litter from my face. My eyes, nose, ears and mouth were clogged with dirt. For several minutes I choked and spat. Searing pains ran through my body, and my skin felt violently scorched.

Groaning and gasping, I opened my eyes, and it was some

175

time before the tears cleared them enough for me to see the tiny scratch of light overhead. For a while it seemed as if I could hear people treading about, and once there came another rumbling noise. Then the sound died.

I began to writhe. "Help! Help me!" I forced out the words with all my strength. They were like a frog's croak. Again and again I called out and then gasped in despair. The pressure was becoming unbearable.

Hours seemed to elapse. I would call, blank out, come to, call, blank out. Gradually a numbness settled and I began trying to visualize what might have happened. A big bomb. The Americans had dropped a new bomb. Was it true? While flying I had heard repeated radio warnings from the enemy in Saipan, admonishing us to surrender, stating that the greatest power the earth had ever known was soon to be unleashed on the land of the rising sun.

What an ironical situation! A suicide pilot dying on the ground, only a short distance from his home! I almost laughed. Such an ignoble way to die!

Perhaps no one would ever dare approach Hiroshima. Maybe all of Japan was gone. Had a B-29 circled over every city, releasing a parachute? What a thought. No more Japan! Everything gone! No, of course not, I was dreaming I gave a start.

Dust had sifted through the hole above, and now it was a mere bird's eye peeping down at me. More dust. The eye closed. I yelled. Feeling as if my lungs might tear loose, I yelled again and again. No answer. Sobbing for air, I made my last feeble bid for help.

A few seconds later the eye blinked at me again, and transformed into a yawning mouth. "Be patient," a voice came. "I'm removing the boards!" Wonderful words. Waiting as I was, the thought came that perhaps I'd been there for days. Was I completely crippled? Would I die a few moments after my release?

Sounds increased—more voices. At length the weight was lifting, darkness changing to light. "Are you all right?" I heard. "Easy, easy—better not move. Better not . . ." I staggered up while the whole world teetered. What a weird, swirling vision! I fell. Arms caught my body, lowering it to earth. Men in white, it seemed.

"What happened?" I creaked.

"We don't know. A new enemy weapon."

"You'll be all right," another said. "Just stay here until you regain your strength. No broken bones. You'll be all right."

They turned to go. "Wait!" I became terrified. "Don't go!"

"We must," came the spectral voices. "Hiroshima is in ruins—everyone dead or dying." Leaving that comforting thought, the blurred figures faded.

"Don't go!" It was no use, and I broke into a painful, dry crying. But the crying itself hurt so much that I stopped and struggled for some degree of sensibility. Not until some time later did I learn that my benefactors, the men in white, were soldiers from the army hospital who had dived under their beds when the explosion occurred, barely escaping destruction themselves. I also learned that I had been buried for nearly six hours—from 8:15 A.M. until 2:00 P.M.

There was no way of determining the extent of my injuries at first, but after about thirty minutes in the open air I struggled to my feet. As I stood swaying, my vision cleared, opening a nightmarish spectacle—a horrifying sight such as I had never seen before—a sight no man must ever see again.

People have attempted to describe Hiroshima after the atomic blast on that fateful August 6, 1945. No one has succeeded, or ever will. What happened was too far beyond the horizon of human experience.

Certain broad pictures burn as vividly in my mind today as they did then—scenes of a great metropolis reduced to a fiery rubble-pit—129,558 human beings killed, crippled or missing—all within a few ticks of a watch.

Standing there, swaying, staring glassily like one demented, I felt moisture. A black rain was settling. For a moment I could not remember how I had come to this place or why. About me, the land was leveled. Cries, groans, and wails emanated from everywhere. Unbelievable! Still, my vision was too blurred to discern people distinctly.

Shiratori Street was buried with houses, folded and strewn like trampled strawberry boxes. Bodies were scattered about. In the distance, a few of the sturdiest buildings still stood, charred and skeletal, some of them listing, ready to topple. Fires rampaged.

Groggily I gazed through the filter of gray toward the sun —nothing but a sickly smear—then at the ground where I'd been buried. Vaguely I realized that once more fate had taken a turn in my favor. A cement water trough used in case of fire, about the size of an office desk, had stood against the house opposite the blast. Falling directly at its base, I had lain in a pocket that formed a right triangle, partially protected from the collapsing walls. Simultaneously, those walls had shielded me from the explosion and the heat wave which had turned nearby grass to ashes. Some of the grass had actually melted. Sand and mortar had settled in the trough, forcing it to overflow. The remaining water had utterly evaporated.

A quick personal examination indicated eyes badly swollen, skin on my hands and arms baked, a bruised right calf, numerous cuts and contusions. As though drunk, I hobbled off with no direction in mind, and within a short distance found a pile of bodies. One or two people were alive, struggling to get free. A blackened form rolled from the heap and a head emerged. The face was singed beef, and its single eye blinked at me. The nose was gone and the mouth writhed soundlessly.

"Here, here, I'll help you," I said, and began dragging away the cadavers. Tugging at a dead arm, I fell backward. The flesh from the elbow down had sloughed off in my hands like the skin of a baked potato, leaving the glistening bone.

Feeling my stomach contract, I continued my task, freeing the prisoner. One or two people assisted, but others merely looked on futilely. The moaning about me had become a horrendous din, and I moved on.

Within seconds I saw a man whose lower half was pinned beneath a beam. Half a dozen people were grunting and prying with levers. As they dragged him free, he emitted one agonized scream and died, blood gushing from his bowels. Hip to ankle, he had been mangled, but the beam's pressure had prevented external bleeding.

Utterly stupefied, I continued. All about me people were moving like half-frozen insects, holding their bodies, clasping their heads. An extraordinary number were naked. A few, mostly women, tried to cover themselves. Others were totally oblivious to their own nudity. I realized that my own clothes were in tatters. My remaining trouser leg, like a thin, dried crust, crumbled apart when I brushed against a jagged board. I reeled on, a wild, glaring animal. I was insane and I knew it—one of those rare instances when a man sees himself in different perspective. I could honestly see myself, the same haggard creature that others were seeing.

Once a woman called to me. She lay on the ground, unable to rise. Attempts to help her were useless, for my slightest touch caused her agony. Her body was blistered past recognition. The hair had been burned to charcoal, and layers of her flesh were peeling off like old wallpaper. One side of her throat was scathed and laid open so that I could see the delicate blood vessels pulsating with tortured blue life. Her lips were trying to form words. What were they? I listened to the dry buzz of her breath, and then understood: "Kill me. Please kill me."

Transfixed, I stared at her, my mouth open wide. The light in those eyes was dying. Suddenly my entire body shook with a great moan. I threw my hands to my face, then staggered to my feet and stumbled on—lost. Innumerable forms appeared, all suffering from the same hideous skin condition. Like lepers, they were falling apart.

Possibly an hour had passed when I found myself before the remains of the Yamanaka Girls' High School. At 8:15 approximately four hundred girls had assembled in rows on the school grounds to receive daily announcements before beginning classes. The blast had scattered them out, stripping off everything but their belts. Watches, rings and buckles had been embedded in their flesh by the heat. The school pendants worn about their necks were burned in between their breasts.

Parents were examining the bodies. I watched a mother bury her face against her husband's chest, watched as their bodies shuddered with sobbing. I saw expressions beyond grief and despair, heard the hysterical wailing, saw blank faces.

Efforts at identification were futile, for the bodies of the four hundred girls were utterly charred. Teeth projected— macabre grins in flattened, featureless faces. The burned odor, like the reek of fertilizer and fish, cloyed in my nostrils and I held my stomach, vomiting.

Some time later I spied an army truck. I ran for it and collapsed. "Wait!" I screamed, "wait!" The truck rolled away, the men in the back blinking at me stupidly. They couldn't even distinguish me from a civilian and I lay where I had fallen, my face in the dirt. Another army truck rumbled by. I raised my hand in a feeble signal, but it went on. No, a hundred yards ahead it had stopped and was backing up. For the third time that day I rose from the earth, and, amazed at my own strength, began to run. I made it to the truck. In a bad state of shock, I crossed the Ota River, heading back toward Hiro. There was a human carpet along those shores, throbbing blotches. Thousands sprawled along the banks as far as I could see, their groans blending in a dreadful dirge.

Countless numbers lay half in the water, trying to cool themselves. Many had died that way, face down. The Ota was filled with living and dead, many of whom had drowned. Corpses bobbed near the shore or washed along with the current. Mothers, fathers, aged and infant—the bomb had used no discrimination.

Then the city fell behind in a crimson haze and once again I was looking out on the fields, unchanged, except that the shadows were now running out from the west instead of the east.

29

THE VOICE OF THE EMPEROR

During the following thirty-six hours I was restricted to my quarters, bedridden. But, wrecked and exhausted though I was, I could find no rest. My body was on fire, my eyes continually smarting and watering. On August 8, having scarcely slept or eaten, I was detailed to fly a Shinshitei, a speedy, two-engine reconnaissance plane, over Hiroshima and the surrounding area.

From 7,000 feet I peered through binoculars, down into the city's heart, much of it still burning. Smoke hung in layers, hiding most of the area. Everywhere havoc, and it was difficult to tell where even the most familiar buildings had stood.

Flooding the roads, in muddy currents, were human beings —fleeing to the mountains and outlying cities: Kaitaichi, Miyajima and Ujina. Occasionally those rivers formed tributaries as military trucks forded through—truckloads of soldiers filing back and forth, evacuating military personnel, fighting fires. What an absurd undertaking it seemed. The great bomb had utterly demolished the Second General Army Headquarters, along with Hiroshima's military supply buildings. Our troops in many areas would soon feel the loss.

Crackling from the radio, words whined: ". . . as yet,

authorities have not determined the exact nature of the force which . . . new bomb . . . doctors investigating but baffled . . ."

I tried another station and heard strains from *Light of the Firefly* (the melody of Auld Lang Syne). Then a familiar voice interrupted: "My dear Japanese pilots. This is Saipan, and I am Japanese as you are. At this moment I am safe from the horror of war, comfortable and well cared-for. Are you, also? Why, my friends, must you continue to be the victims of a senseless war? You gallant *Kamikaze* who daily sacrifice your lives—to what avail? Why must you be victimized? Why must you die?" He went on to ask us if we comprehended fully what had happened again at Nagasaki, this very day! America, the voice said, could offer only one alternative—surrender or annihilation. "Do you know that your mothers, your wives, your sisters, your children are now starving—all because of the diabolical selfishness of a few men in Tokyo?"

To surrender we would need only to waggle our wings upon approaching an American landing field. "I will be back with you in two hours," the voice informed us. *Old Kentucky Home,* a song popular among the Japanese, was then played.

Many times I had felt the nostalgia of such songs, the desire to stop fighting—times when nothing mattered but peace, peace under almost any conditions. Indeed I had even gone so far as to plot a detailed escape from Hiro. In any escape plans, fuel presented the main problem. I had considered knocking the guard unconscious during the night, then donning his uniform to transfer gasoline from the drums to my fighter with buckets. If anyone were to accost me during the process of removal, I would simply say that a drum was leaking, that I had been ordered to transfer the fuel. Once tanked up and in the air, heading for Saipan, no one would be able to stop me. I was confident of that.

But now . . . staring down into the death and devastation that was once Hiroshima, learning that the enemy had now demolished Nagasaki . . . now, even though the man from Saipan had spoken the truth, I wanted to lay hold of his throat. I hated the enemy with a passion. Had an American plane appeared, I would have done everything in my power to crash it. My own life was of no importance.

Two hours of flying had dulled my sight, and sleep began swelling in at me. My stomach was beginning to growl. My skin was peeling off, my hands and face puffy. The combination was too much; the weariness would drag me under. I radioed in and was granted permission to return.

Upon landing I made my report and sagged off to the barrack. Inside, several of the radical *Kichigai* flyers were arguing heatedly with the *Sukebei* about the status of the war. Russia's belated decision to take up arms against us was creating consternation. Russia, in my opinion, had played a cunning and avaricious game—like a vulture, who attacks to satisfy his gluttony once the eagle has dealt the deathblow. Now Russia could share in the spoils of war with the Americans, but she would not actually be hated as they would. Few Japanese a decade or more from now could remember that Soviet boots had helped to tramp out our death rattle.

Too enervated to join in the arguments, however, I crumpled on my cot, not even bothering to undress, oblivious to everything for the next fifteen hours.

During the next few days my skin grew worse. The epidermis on all the exposed areas was sloughing off, while parts of the under surface decayed, smelling nauseous. My face had broken into a rash and was covered with boils, prelude to a lengthy illness which later kept me bald for months, and a radiation ailment which still lingers.

At the medical dispensary, doctors eyed me furtively, as though I were in the advanced stages of bubonic plague, and offered little help. One of them suggested that my burns were simply the result of heat, that my fever was aggravated by a cold. His perfunctory advice was: "Soak your face in a pail of water from time to time. It will be all right."

All suicide missions had been temporarily canceled by the *Daihonei* and, despite the good doctor's unconcern, my condition was now serious enough to keep me even from flying reconnaissance. Nothing to do but wait now. Throughout the base tension was growing. The combination of hope and fear produced a new kind of anxiety. Our nerves were like fine crystal in a bouncing truck bed, our actions spastic. Day and night my body tingled. Whenever I lay down, my muscles twitched, and at times I trembled all over.

On August 14, a friend rushed into the barrack. He'd just returned from a reconnaissance. "Kuwahara!" he whispered. "They say we will surrender tomorrow! The emperor will announce Japan's surrender! The air is full of it!"

Swiftly the rumor spread. The tension increased. That night few men slept at Hiro.

At noon the next day officers and men were assembled in the mess hall before the radio, mute as stones. Static drowned out some of the words, but others were audible enough for us to determine what was happening. Our emperor was offically announcing the surrender of Japan!

His proclamation, like the atomic flash, left everyone stunned, and it was an instant before the explosion occurred. I looked at the stricken faces, watched the expressions alter. Suddenly a cry went up and one of the *Kichigai* leaped to his feet. "Those American *chikusyo!* May God condemn them! Revenge! Revenge! Are we women? Let us strike this very moment—before it is too late! We are expendable!" His gesture sent cups crashing from the table.

"We are expendable!" rose the cry. A score of men sprang up and would have rushed to their planes had not the commander intervened.

After we had returned to our barracks, motors groaned overhead—the screech of diving planes, followed by two sharp explosions. We rushed forth to see flames crackling on the airstrip. Sergeants Kashiwabara and Kinoshita had quietly sneaked to their planes and become some of the first Japanese to suffer death rather than the humiliation of surrender.

The deaths precipitated bitter arguing. Men from the *Sukebei* faction contended, naturally enough, that it was stupid to fight any longer, that nothing could be gained by dying. The words had come from our emperor. The *Kichigai*, on the other hand, maintained that life would not be worth living, that the Americans would torture and kill us anyway. The least we could do, they said, would be to avenge the terrible crimes at Hiroshima and Nagasaki.

Corporal Yoshida was the most adamant of all. After a fiery argument, he rushed from the barrack, ranting and cursing. A moment later his frenetic voice sounded outside: "You rotten, cowardly bastards!" Pistol shots ripped through the walls. We peered outside to see him lying in a widening, crimson pool. He had used the final bullet on himself.

A wave of suicides followed. Several officers placed pistols in their mouths as Yoshida had done, and squeezed the triggers. Men committed *harakiri*, bit off their own tongues, cut their throats, or hanged themselves.

That same day Admiral Matoi Ugaki, commander of the navy's Fifth Air Fleet, and several of his echelon, became some of the war's final *Kamikaze*. In a calm, fixed manner they taxied their Suisei bombers down the strip at Oita and were last seen heading into the clouds for Okinawa. Vice-Admiral Takijiro Onishi, "Father of the *Tokkotai*," having confessed to an overwhelming sense of guilt, committed *hara-kiri*. Other high-ranking officials followed his lead.

On the morning of the 18th, Hiro's commanding officer announced that the propellers were being removed from our planes. All arms and ammunition, except enough for the guards, had been placed under lock and key. His face was weary as he said, "You are all aware now that we have received orders to refrain from further aggression. Regardless of our own personal feelings, there will be no more fighting. Japan has lost the war. The time has come for us to consider the future—to face reality. Our emperor has spoken." The tears flowed, unashamed, down his cheeks. In a moment two

The ensuing days were perhaps the strangest in Japan's hundred broken men were weeping.

military history. The inequality which had so long existed between officers and men disappeared. Officers who had dealt unjustly with their men fled by night and were never heard of again. Others were killed trying to escape. More than one man deserted, hoping to gain anonymity among the civilians before the Americans took over. Records, documents, names of air force personnel—all were destroyed to prevent identification by the enemy.

Heavy guard was posted around warehouses and installations to prevent robbery by military personnel and even civilians who ferreted through the fences. Violence flared throughout the base. *Kichigai* and *Sukebei* bickered and carried on gang wars. I refrained from the arguments as much as possible, biding my time, wondering. I had seen enough conflict.

It was on the 21st that I read the bulletin board near the mess hall. The board looked no different—still the same white notices. But the words! "The following men are to be discharged, effective 23 August." Part way down the list was "Cpl. Kuwahara, Yasuo."

It was as if someone had knocked the breath from me. Somehow I felt that it was all a mistake. But it was true—my discharge was soon confirmed. It was true!

In two days I would be a free man. I simply could not believe it—that it would be all over. Incredulity gripped me, and I drifted about the base, nearly demented, shaking my head, muttering to myself. Wasn't it true that at Kochi and Oita airfields they had not yet taken propellers from their planes? And weren't efforts being made by our military diehards to continue the war? Certain factions were propagating the idea that Japan had not actually surrendered, that she had merely reached a tentative agreement with the Allies. Stupid, blind fools! Undoubtedly such individuals had not smelled the stench of Hiroshima and Nagasaki.

And here at Hiro secret meetings were held by the two rival groups. If the *Kichigai* element became dominant . . . well, there was still danger. I was still awaiting a set of death orders.

More than ten years later I learned that on August 8, 1945, I was to have been part of a final desperation attack, involving thousands of men and planes—all that was left. The great bomb that had destroyed so many of my countrymen had saved me.

30

THE FAREWELL CUP

Despite my qualms, the remaining days passed more calmly than I'd anticipated. Early on the 23rd of August, I donned a new uniform. For a long time I looked at myself in the mirror—at the golden eagle patches on my shoulders. I was looking into an unfamiliar face, at an unfamiliar being. After the long months, the months that were to have ended somewhere in the Pacific, I was going to be free. Free! "It's all over. It's all over." The words repeated themselves endlessly.

And yet a wistfulness was creeping over me. Scenes were sweeping before me in a changing panorama. I was looking through that mirror into the past—burning cities and dead men, planes, clouds, sky, ships and the infinite sea. Voices were calling. Pressing my head against the glass, I closed my eyes.

Tingling strangely, I left the barracks and, as though compelled by another mind, wandered out onto the empty airstrip. From somewhere the sounds of ancient music drifted, very faintly. At a far corner Hiro's once proud fighter planes huddled, emasculated without their propellers.

Crossing the field slowly, I moved among them and found my Hayabusa. I leaned on a patched wing for a moment, then climbed into the cockpit and grasped the controls. Cold controls. Once I shut my eyes, listening, listening to the fading drone of planes along the red horizon—a muffled roar that gradually simmered and was gone. I started. There was nothing. There had been nothing.

By 10 A.M. I had bidden my last farewell, saluted the waving flag—still the flag with its rising sun—and passed beyond the gates of Hiro forever.

Going home. Never before had life been so dreamlike. I was among a people strange even to myself. As yet the enemy had taken no unfair advantage of our surrender. And, surprisingly enough to many of the Americans, the people at large were already resigned to a new order. The emperor had spoken. They were a laughing people because of their relief, a crying people because of their joy, their bitterness and their sorrow. Many awaited the invasion with trepidation. Others merely felt curiosity. But more than anything, there was a growing happiness. The war had ended.

As the truck rumbled along, I sighed and began to breathe deeply. My skin was still peeling, my eyes still burned, and the fever from August 6th had not entirely abated. But it didn't matter—not then. Idly I traced my fingers over a tiny cut on my hand and began thinking of the farewell gathering I had attended the night before. A dozen friends had convened for a *sukiyaki* dinner in the billet of a Lieutenant Kurotsuka. There had been toasting with *sake,* and each man had cut his own hand and drunk the blood of his comrade's in a token of brotherhood.

Kurotsuka, an assistant commander for the Second Squadron, had been a peace-lover but a valiant leader, beloved by all his men. I kept seeing the ruddy face, the keen, knowing eyes, and kept remembering his final words as he stood before us:

"We have lost a material war—but spiritually we shall never be vanquished. Let us not lose our spirit of brotherhood and let us never lose the spirit of Japan.

"We are aged men in one sense. And yet we are very young, and the future stretches before us. It is for us now to dedicate ourselves not to death—but to life—to the rebuilding of Japan, that she may one day be a great power, yet stand respected as a power for good by every nation.

"For what men, my comrades, in all this world, will ever know war as we have known it? Or what men will ever cherish peace as we shall cherish it?"

The *sake* cups were raised high.

The most fascinating people and events of World War II